"When three great minds like these collaborate, a prism is created through which a light of wisdom can shine in the darkest of places. A must-read for all people touched by this unfathomable dilemma."

—**Judge Michele Lowrance (ret)**, mediator and author of *The Good Karma Divorce* and *Parental Alienation 911*

"In each journey through parental alienation, it is easy to lose the way. What seems to be a clear and just path in navigating family court is not always reality. Amy J. L. Baker, Brian Ludmer, and J. Michael Bone have given alienated parents a comprehensive road map that allows them to make their journey through this highly emotional period with level heads and hearts. The authors' work empowers readers and leaves them feeling revived, secure, and confident as they travel to their final destination: reunification with their children."

—**Jill Egizii**, president of the Parental Alienation Awareness Organization, USA

Register your **new harbinger** titles for additional benefits!

When you register your **new harbinger** title—purchased in any format, from any source—you get access to benefits like the following:

- Downloadable accessories like printable worksheets and extra content

- Instructional videos and audio files

- Information about updates, corrections, and new editions

Not every title has accessories, but we're adding new material all the time.

Access free accessories in 3 easy steps:

1. Sign in at NewHarbinger.com (or **register** to create an account).

2. Click on **register a book**. Search for your title and click the **register** button when it appears.

3. Click on the **book cover or title** to go to its details page. Click on **accessories** to view and access files.

That's all there is to it!

If you need help, visit:

NewHarbinger.com/accessories

new harbinger
CELEBRATING
40 YEARS

THE

HIGH-CONFLICT CUSTODY BATTLE

Protect Yourself & Your Kids from a Toxic Divorce, False Accusations & Parental Alienation

Amy J. L. Baker, PhD

J. Michael Bone, PhD

Brian Ludmer, BComm, LLB

New Harbinger Publications, Inc.

Publisher's Note

Distributed in Canada by Raincoast Books

Copyright © 2014 by Amy J. L. Baker, Michael J. Bone, and Brian Ludmer
New Harbinger Publications, Inc.
5674 Shattuck Avenue
Oakland, CA 94609
www.newharbinger.com

Cover design by Amy Shoup
Acquired by Melissa Kirk
Edited by Will Derooy

Library of Congress Cataloging-in-Publication Data

Baker, Amy J. L., author.
  The high-conflict custody battle : protect yourself and your kids from a toxic divorce, false accusations, and parental alienation / Amy J. L. Baker, J. Michael Bone, Brian Ludmer.
      pages cm
  Includes bibliographical references.
  ISBN 978-1-62625-073-4 (paperback) -- ISBN 978-1-62625-074-1 (pdf e-book) -- ISBN 978-1-62625-075-8 (epub) 1. Custody of children--United States. 2. Parent and child (Law)--United States. 3. Divorce--Law and legislation--United States. 4. Children of divorced parents--United States. 5. Parental alienation syndrome. 6. Psychological child abuse. I. Bone, J. Michael, author. II. Ludmer, Brian, author. III. Title.
  KF547.B35 2014
  346.7301'73--dc23
                            2014016748

Printed in the United States of America

16   15   14

10   9   8   7   6   5   4   3   2   1   First printing

We dedicate this book to our families, from whom we have learned so much about love, respect, and compassion, and to parents and children affected by high-conflict custody disputes and loyalty conflicts. May they find a way to remain connected despite the forces pulling them apart.

Contents

Acknowledgments

We gratefully acknowledge the wonderful team at New Harbinger Publications, who create a collaborative writing and editing process, including Melissa Kirk and Jess Beebe, and freelance copyeditor Will DeRooy. The book has been greatly improved through their keen attention to the words and their meaning, ensuring that the book would speak to the broadest range of parents.

Introduction

About half of all marriages end in divorce. Although most divorcing couples aspire to attain a "good divorce"—defined as both parents working together to raise their children cooperatively—some parents are not so lucky. For those parents, the postdivorce period is marked by a high degree of conflict with their former spouse and frequent if not ongoing legal wrangling over the children's health, education, and welfare. These parents are involved in what is known as a high-conflict custody dispute, in which there is ongoing disagreement and acrimony, inability to resolve conflicts outside of court, and failure to see eye to eye on almost every aspect of their children's upbringing. The conflict that existed in the marriage is carried over if not exacerbated in the postdivorce phase.

If you have been to court over custody of your children several times and your case file is several inches thick, this book is for you. This book is also for you if you are engaged in ongoing legal action regarding your parenting time (access to your children, visitation with your children) as well as your rights to help make decisions about your children's health, education, and welfare.

It is difficult to imagine a more stressful situation for a parent than being in a high-conflict custody dispute. Not only are you dealing with an ex who may be undermining and interfering with your relationship with your children, but also you have to navigate the complexities and intricacies of the legal and mental health systems. A high-conflict custody dispute can be like a black hole that sucks away vast amounts of your money, happiness, and energy.

As legal and mental health professionals, we work with parents like you every day. Because we understand the heartache, frustration, worry, anxiety, uncertainty, and pain you are experiencing, we have decided to pool our practical experience in order to share with you some of what we have learned over the years.

One thing we know from working with parents like you is that you probably have an ongoing list of concerns about your relationship with your children, on top of which are a series of practical questions about how to find the right attorney or mental health professional for your case and how to work effectively with the attorneys and psychologists you come into contact with. These questions may include:

- Do I have the best attorney for my situation?

- How can I present my evidence to my attorney so that she understands my concerns?

- How can I explain my situation to the court so that the judge understands my concerns?

- How can I describe my concerns to the custody evaluator without bad-mouthing my ex?

- Do I need an expert witness? If so, how do I find the right one?

- What are custody evaluators looking for when deciding what is in my children's best interest?

- Is my ex trying to turn the children against me? If so, what can I do about it?

This book is intended neither to replace the advice of an attorney (far from it!) nor to provide you with all the emotional support and psychological guidance you might need. But we do aim to lighten your load by providing you with some "big picture" ideas along with a lot of "nuts and bolts" to help you deal with a high-conflict custody dispute. We hope to help you be prepared for what lies ahead so that you can do your best to protect yourself and your children from this terrible plight.

Whether you realize it or not, in this (postdivorce) phase of your life, you will be experiencing a lot of stress, if not trauma, in various forms, which can make it difficult for you to make the most informed decisions about your family, your finances, and your future. You might be tempted to let anger, fear, or frustration dictate your responses to certain situations, but that could get in the way of your goal of protecting your children and preserving your relationship with them. If you follow the advice presented in this book, you will be better able to manage both your high-conflict custody dispute and the emotions it triggers in you.

There are several key themes throughout the book. One is the importance of having the "right" professionals on your team. At a minimum, you need an attorney who truly understands your situation and how to deal with it effectively in the courts. If your current attorney has allowed your ex and opposing counsel to institute continual delays in the process, has urged you to plead guilty or no contest to domestic violence to make the problem "go away," or cannot articulate a theory of your case and a compelling counter to your ex's behaviors and accusations, then this person is probably not the right attorney for you. We will discuss selecting the best attorney for you in chapter 3.

We focus throughout the book on the potential utility of other experts on your team—including a mental health consultant to help you select the right attorney, to prepare your witnesses, and to hold your hand and guide you through the various phases of the custody dispute. You might also benefit from retaining an expert witness to explain your ex's interfering or undermining behavior to the courts, rebut a custody evaluation, or critique an abuse investigation. If selected properly, these experts can articulate your issues and concerns in a compelling fashion for the judge. You can find information about mental health consultants in chapter 4 and about expert witnesses in chapter 7.

We also emphasize the importance of being your own best advocate and becoming educated about your options and your choices. This is especially true with respect to deciding whether to initiate a legal action with the court (assuming that your ex hasn't already filed one). You must be aware of what legal actions you can take and the likely outcomes, benefits, and disadvantages of each. You can find out this information by educating yourself and discussing your case with legal professionals and consultants. The last thing you want to do is file a motion frivolously or initiate a legal action that could waste time and money or be likely to have an unfavorable outcome. Likewise, you don't want lack of information to cause you to miss an important window of opportunity to file a motion. It is also essential that you be informed about the various types of custody arrangements and parenting plans available to parents in the jurisdiction (e.g., county or region) in which your case will be heard and the differences among them. You must conduct your own legal research and consult with professionals to ensure that you understand the various terms and their implications for you and your children. This is especially true if you believe that your ex is actively attempting to undermine your relationship with your children. You must become very knowledgeable about the issues that are relevant to your case, and your attorney must be an expert as well. Don't make the mistake of assuming that simply being an attorney or even a family law attorney makes anyone an expert on your particular type of case. Custody and time-sharing decisions are made by assessing parents' interest in, aptitude for, knowledge of, and style of parenting against the specific needs of the family's children. It is important to demonstrate good skills and knowledge. Reading books on parenting and taking parenting classes are always helpful.

In chapter 5, we will discuss the topic of evidence preparation, especially the importance of preparing and organizing your evidence for the attorney, the custody evaluator, and any expert witnesses in an objective and balanced fashion that will facilitate their work on your case. There are multiple ways to organize your evidence, and it is essential that each expert receives the documents she needs in the manner in which she needs them. When preparing your evidence, you should be balanced and objective about your and your ex's strengths and weaknesses.

It is essential that you be mindful at all times of the impression you are creating (to the judge, to the custody evaluator, to your children's friends, and to the community) and work very hard to remain calm and authentic, even if your ex is vilifying you. Be aware of the possibility that your ex is spreading poisonous messages about you, and if she is, make sure that your demeanor, actions, and choices don't confirm those messages. Impression management is extremely important in custody evaluations, and we will cover this topic in depth in chapter 7.

Throughout the book, we will remind you to make sure that your attorney has a theory of your case that emphasizes that your parenting is normative (within the normal bounds of what is considered good and proper care). You need to create an emotional connection with the judge and the custody evaluator through the details, stories, and pictures you share so that you can convey to them the bond you share (or shared, if distance has entered into your relationship) with your children.

There are legal and mental health remedies that you can request of the court, and you should be aware of the advantages and disadvantages of, as well as the judge's comfort level with, each of them. We'll help you resist settling for options that are doomed to fail. At the same time, it is important that you manage your expectations and understand that reversal of custody (that is, going from your ex's having full custody to your having full custody, which you might strongly believe is necessary in your situation) can be hard to achieve. We will explore the topic of remedies in chapter 9.

You might believe that your ex is trying to turn your children against you by manipulating them to unjustifiably reject you, or that your children are currently alienated from you. If so, it is important to understand how the process of alienation works and how you can describe what is going on so that the legal and mental health professionals involved in your case will also understand. This topic is also addressed throughout the book.

A central message woven throughout the book is the importance of taking care of yourself, especially if you are a "targeted parent," meaning you are facing a hostile ex who is interfering with and undermining your relationship with your children. Some targeted parents are blessed with a loving and supportive circle of friends and family who rally behind them; others are surrounded by people who shame and blame them for what has happened. It is essential that you reach out to others who understand and can support you in what you are going through. A high-conflict custody dispute is not something you want to go through alone. Regardless, no one will experience the ups and downs of your custody drama as intensely as you do, so you must be mindful of how you are doing and feeling along the way. Build in time to take care of yourself (whatever that means to you) on days that are likely to be even more stressful than usual—days on which you have an interview with the custody evaluator or an appearance in court, for example, or important days such as holidays or milestones you can't share with your child). It is essential that you take care of your physical, emotional, and spiritual health at all times, because dealing with a hostile ex and a high-conflict custody dispute is both a sprint and a marathon, requiring extraordinary internal as well as external resources. We will provide you with tips and resources in chapter 2 and throughout the book to help you take good care of yourself.

We extend our heartfelt sympathies to you as a parent faced with a high-conflict custody dispute, and we offer the lessons we have learned in the field to provide you with some essential tools and tips to make this experience as manageable as possible and increase the chances of a positive outcome for you and your children.

CHAPTER 1

High-Conflict Custody Disputes and Litigation: An Overview

The term "high-conflict custody dispute" refers to situations in which separated or divorced parents are engaged in an ongoing dispute about parental rights and responsibilities (in essence, parenting time and decision making). Typically, one parent wants to limit the children's access to and relationship with the other parent, sometimes based on accusations of abuse, neglect, or seriously deficient parenting. At the same time, the accused parent believes that he is being maligned and unfairly denied access to the children. High-conflict custody disputes may also involve one parent wanting to move to another state or province or outside the municipality of residence; accusations of sexual or physical abuse or domestic violence; and disagreements about specific aspects of the children's health, education, and welfare (which school the children should attend, what medical care they should receive, etc.). In a high-conflict custody dispute, long-standing differences bring the parties back to court over a period of several years, with little success in resolving them since consenusal or mediated resolutions have not worked.

High-conflict custody disputes represent a small fraction of all divorces, but they take up the vast majority of family court resources. And, of course, for a parent in a high-conflict custody dispute, the process can take up vast amounts of energy, money, and time. Moreover, elements of high-conflict custody disputes may be present in any custody dispute (e.g., some concern that your ex will bad-mouth you to the children, some concern that you will be denied parenting time).

Types of Custody

All custody disputes involve a disagreement about some aspect of custody, so it is important for you to understand what that means from a legal standpoint. First, there are two types of custody with respect to children: physical (also known as residential) and legal (i.e., decision making). Physical/residential custody is the term used to describe the living and sleeping arrangements of children and which parent is responsible for the child on a day-to-day basis. For example, if one parent has physical/residential custody of the children on a given day, that is the person with whom the children should be that day and who decides what the children eat for breakfast, when they do their homework, and so forth.

There are two basic types of physical/residential custody: sole and shared. If one parent has sole physical/residential custody, then the other parent may have what is referred to as "parenting time" or "visitation" with the children. If the two parents have shared physical/residential custody, then each parent has "parenting time." Shared does not necessarily mean equal (50/50) in terms of time. Shared could describe any amount of time that the two parents agree upon or the court orders. The schedule of the children's time with each parent (which parent has responsibility for the children on which days) is spelled out in a parenting plan. The parents can agree upon a parenting plan, or a parenting plan can be court ordered. Some plans are very specific and explain exactly how holidays and vacations will be allocated; others are less detailed. There are many different types of shared parenting time arrangements. Popular ones include one parent having primary residential custody and the other parent having parenting time every other weekend and one overnight a week. Another shared plan is for the children to spend 50 percent of their time with each parent. There are different types of 50/50 time arrangements. For example, in some arrangements, each parent has the children for seven consecutive days; others follow a "2-5-5-2" pattern, in which the children spend two days with Parent A, then five with Parent B, then five with Parent A, then two with Parent B. Parenting plan schedules can change over the summer and other school holidays, so even parents who have parenting time only every other weekend during the school year may have parenting time for half of the summer or other school holidays. The same holds true of holidays and vacations, which can be shared equally even when one parent has sole physical/residential custody for the school year. There is no state, provincial, or federal law that spells out how a parenting plan should work, so there is wide latitude from jurisdiction to jurisdiction in how parenting plans are designed. There is a general trend in the direction of time sharing (rather than one parent having primary custody and the other having visitation).

Legal custody refers to the authority to make decisions regarding the children's health, education, and welfare (selection of schools, medical care, religious upbringing, etc.). Legal custody may be separate from residential custody. For example, one parent may have sole residential custody but still share legal custody with the other parent. Shared legal custody seems to be fairly common, even in high-conflict families of divorce.

What is often not spelled out in parenting plans is what happens when two parents who share legal custody disagree (on which school the children should attend, which pediatrician they should go to, etc.). Often, if one parent has primary residential custody, that parent ultimately makes the decisions, with the presumption that she is the parent who knows the children best. Thus, even if you have joint legal custody, it may not result in actually having an equal voice in your children's upbringing, unless you and your ex can cooperate or happen to agree on the major issues. There are also variations on sole or shared legal custody. For example, one parent may have sole legal custody but be prohibited from doing certain things that most legal custodians can do, such as moving away or changing the children's last name.

It is essential, as you consider your own custody conflict, that you know what terms are used in your jurisdiction, what they mean, and what the legal implications are for you. For example, in some jurisdictions there is a presumption of shared custody; in others there is not. Your attorney and mental health consultant can help educate you in this regard.

Common Areas of Contention in High-Conflict Custody Disputes

Although Tolstoy wrote that every unhappy family is unhappy in its own way, there are some common issues around which most high-conflict custody disputes revolve. The first is enforcement of parenting time. Typically, in a high-conflict custody dispute, one parent is not producing the children when he is supposed to (e.g., not dropping them off at the appointed time, canceling visits, saying the children don't want to visit). Many high-conflict custody disputes involve a motion to enforce the current parenting plan. That is, there is an actual court order that specifies each parent's parenting time, but one parent has decided to not follow the plan, and the other is requesting that the court compel him to follow the current plan.

A second issue occurs when one parent wants to move away with the children and the other parent objects. In some jurisdictions, there is a requirement to obtain court approval prior to a move away with the children, but some parents plan to move anyway, and that may compel the other parent to file a motion to prevent it if the move would preclude the "left behind" parent from having regular and ongoing custody and being involved on a routine basis in the children's day-to-day lives.

A third issue common in high-conflict custody disputes is one parent wants to terminate the other parent's parenting time (i.e., to legally change the parenting time) based on a claim that the children do not want to go and/or that the other parent is abusive and should not be allowed access to the children. This is often but not always accompanied by a complaint being filed with child protection services to initiate a child abuse investigation.

A fourth common scenario is when one parent files a motion to increase her parenting time based on the fact that the children are older and presumably able to handle more time away from the other parent, or based on some other change in circumstance (e.g., the parent who is filing the motion has changed her schedule and is able to accommodate more parenting time, has moved closer to the children and can have more frequent visits).

A fifth common scenario involves claims of parental alienation, a term that is widely used among warring parents. Parental alienation describes a family dynamic in which one parent believes the other parent is behaving in a manner that is likely to turn the children against him. Other terms used interchangeably include gatekeeping, hostile aggressive parenting, and visitation interference. In the book *Co-Parenting with a Toxic Ex*, Amy Baker and Paul Fine (2014a) describe seventeen primary parental alienation strategies, which they organize into five overarching categories of concerning behaviors that the "alienating" or "favored" parent may engage in against the "targeted" or "rejected" parent:

1. Poisonous messages in which the alienating parent tries to convince the children that the targeted parent is unloving, unsafe, and unavailable (Poisonous messages may also involve vilifying the targeted parent to the child's community so that other people will validate the message.)

2. Interfering with the targeted parent's contact and communication with the children, which includes blocking messages, limiting parenting time, and reducing the targeted parent's opportunities to show himself to be a safe, loving, and available parent

3. Erasing and replacing the targeted parent, which involves rewriting the children's history with that parent to convince the children that the targeted parent was not loving

and involved, installing a replacement parent to supplant the targeted parent in the children's hearts and minds, and creating an identity for the children that does not involve a meaningful connection with the targeted parent

4. Encouraging the children to betray the targeted parent (e.g., having the children spy on and keep secrets from the targeted parent, allowing or forcing the children to reject the targeted parent in order to create conflict and hurt feelings)

5. Undermining the targeted parent's parental authority and rules of the home while encouraging the children to be dependent on the alienating parent (e.g., encouraging the children to disregard the targeted parent's parenting guidance and encouraging the children to refer to that parent by his first name)

Each of these behaviors creates conflict and a psychological wedge between the children and the targeted parent.

It is hard to imagine a high-conflict custody dispute that doesn't have one or more of the preceding elements, and many have more than one. For example, Parent A believes that Parent B is trying to alienate the children from him, while Parent B claims that Parent A is abusive and the children don't want to see him; or Parent A wants to move away with the children after Parent B moved closer and filed a motion to increase parenting time.

Exercise 1.1: Your Current Situation

As you begin to think about your current situation, it may help to ask yourself the following questions to clarify where you are and where you want to be. Write down your answers on a piece of paper (e.g., in a notebook or journal), or talk them through with a trusted friend.

1. What are your current legal rights as outlined in a court order (if you have a court order)?

2. How satisfied are you with your rights as they are specified in the court order (if you have a court order)?

3. Are you able to exercise all of your parenting rights as they are currently determined in the order (if you have an order) or in your ad hoc parenting plan? If not, what specific rights are you not able to exercise, in terms of parenting time and making decisions about your children's health, education, and welfare?

4. Are you concerned based on your ex's actions and attitudes that she may try to undermine and interfere in your relationship with your children?

5. Are you concerned based on your children's actions and attitudes that they are caught in a loyalty conflict and appear to be siding with your ex?

6. Are you concerned that your ex will (if she hasn't already) want to move away with the children?

7. Are you concerned that your ex will (if he hasn't already) make false allegations of abuse against you?

8. Are you satisfied with the implementation of the parenting plan with respect to transition times and locations, the effect of the children's extracurricular activities on your parenting time, the number of requests for changes by your ex, and your ex's accommodation of your requests for changes?

9. Are you concerned about the degree of hostility that your ex expresses toward you and the negative environment your ex creates at events that you both reasonably have a right to be at?

Your answers to the above questions will serve to indicate whether you are generally satisfied with your current situation or whether you have some serious concerns that you should discuss with an attorney in order to start the legal process of seeking remedy from the court.

When to Seek Legal Remedy

There are three primary times when you will need to seek legal advice. The first is when your ex has initiated a legal proceeding against you that you are generally in agreement with. For example, your ex wants to move away with the children, and you are in principle amenable to this, but you have some questions or concerns. For example, if in the future your ex wants to move even farther away, who will be responsible for transporting the children for your parenting time, and can you have longer visits since they will presumably be less frequent? Even if you agree with what your ex is asking for, you still need to do so in a legally proper manner, which most likely entails hiring an attorney to guide you through the process.

A second scenario in which you need to seek legal advice is when your ex has initiated a legal proceeding asking the court to take some action that you are not in agreement with. Perhaps your ex wants to move away and you don't agree with the move. Perhaps your ex has filed a motion to limit or terminate your parenting time and you don't want your parenting time limited or terminated. Perhaps your ex has filed a motion for the court to assign the children an attorney and you don't think that is a good decision. You will need to explain in a response why the court should not grant your ex's request. You can also add your own requests for court actions when you do so.

A third case in which you will want to seek legal advice is when your ex has not initiated a legal proceeding against you, but you want to initiate a legal proceeding of your own asking the court to take action on your behalf. Perhaps your ex has enrolled your child in therapy or a new school and didn't tell you, and you don't agree with his choice. Perhaps your ex has canceled your parenting time several visits in a row, and you are concerned about this pattern of noncompliance with the court order. Perhaps you believe that the children need therapy, but your ex has denied approval for them to receive counseling.

Exercise 1.2: Developing a Goal for Your Custody Situation

When thinking about what kind of legal proceeding to initiate, you need to consider what your goals are. Use the following questions to help you understand what your goals are and explain them to your attorney. You can write your answers on a piece of paper (e.g., in a notebook or journal).

Satisfaction with Your Current Arrangements

Are you satisfied with the amount of parenting time you have?

Are you satisfied with the parenting schedule (days and times)?

Are you satisfied with the parenting transition locations?

Do you have a desire or plan to move away with the children?

Satisfaction with Implementation of Current Parenting Plan

Does your ex intrude on or interfere with your parenting time?

Does your ex interfere with and undermine your relationship with the children?

Are you concerned about your ex moving away with the children?

Concerns About Your Children's Safety

Are you concerned that your ex is abusing/neglecting the children?

Are you concerned that your ex's significant other is abusing/neglecting the children?

Are you concerned that your ex is not supporting the children's health, education, and welfare?

Use your answers to these questions to help you formulate goals about maintaining, restoring, strengthening, and protecting your relationship with your children. The questions below can guide you.

Where do you want to be in five years with respect to your relationship with your children?

Do you feel hopeful that you will actually have this experience?

If not, what do you see as the major barriers?

What needs to change for you to reach your parenting goals?

Divorce and separation can be very stressful, and it is important that you stay in touch with your emotional well-being to ensure that your emotions don't lead you to make choices that could be harmful to you or your children. So, ask yourself the following questions:

Is anger at or a desire to punish or get revenge against your ex playing a role in your legal strategy?

Are you unreasonably fearful of your ex's ability to properly care for the children because of your own need for control, your bias (e.g., that fathers cannot possibly parent as well as mothers), or your own history?

Is your current emotional state (e.g., sadness, loneliness, fear of being alone, similar negative emotions) motivating you?

If you answered yes to any of the last three questions, we suggest that you refer to chapter 2 to help you explore and process your emotions so that you can act in the best interests of your children. It is important that revenge and a desire to punish your ex not be your underlying motivations. If they are, we strongly recommend that you rethink your legal strategy.

Initiating a legal proceeding with the court is time consuming, expensive, and stressful. Any involvement with the court drains you and your family of emotional and financial resources. You should have a reasonable expectation of prevailing and a strong moral conviction that should you prevail, there will be a positive outcome for you and your children. Make sure that you let your attorney know that you want a realistic assessment of your chances of prevailing (bearing in mind that your attorney needs to be paid no matter the outcome of your case). There are, however, situations in which you might initiate a legal action despite knowing that you will not prevail, for the purposes of creating a court record of your concerns. An example is filing a motion to enforce visitation despite knowing that the judge might not be compelled on the first motion to sanction your ex. The reason to file such a motion is to lay the groundwork for future motions to deal with the pattern of noncompliance that you are experiencing.

A Note About Parental Alienation and Parental Alienation Syndrome (PAS)

In some cases, high-conflict custody disputes involve parental alienation (the efforts on the part of one parent to foster a child's unjustified rejection of the other parent), which can lead to parental alienation syndrome, or PAS (a set of behaviors in children who have been manipulated to unjustifiably reject a parent). We want this book to be as useful as possible for the broadest audience, so we don't limit our discussion of high-conflict custody disputes to cases of parental alienation, but much of the content will apply to cases of parental alienation.

Unfortunately, not all legal and mental health professionals understand what parental alienation is. Therefore, we encourage you to use descriptive terms when discussing your situation with your attorney, with mental health experts, and with custody evaluators. For example, rather than saying, "My ex is engaging in parental alienation," you can say, "I am concerned that my ex is denigrating me and making it difficult for my children to contact me when they are with her." The more specific you can be about your concerns, the more the person you are speaking with will understand what you are talking about. Rather than labeling your ex or your children, describe the behavior that you think is a problem. For example, you may want to think about your ex's behavior in terms of "helpful and supportive co-parenting" versus "unhelpful and unsupportive." Information about parental alienation is presented throughout the book as necessary.

Conclusion

Given that you are in a high-conflict custody dispute, you are probably stressed and concerned about your relationship with your children and about how you are going to effectively interact with the legal and mental health professionals your family will come into contact with. This book was written to provide you with the guidance and resources to help you be an effective advocate on behalf of yourself and your children.

CHAPTER 2

Coping with a High-Conflict Custody Dispute: Taking Care of Yourself

We don't have to tell you that going through a high-conflict custody dispute is like living within a nightmare, a nightmare that seems to never end. You most likely have high levels of anxiety, depression, fear, shame, loneliness, and worry. This is normal. That doesn't mean, however, that you couldn't benefit from counseling to help you cope, and we suggest that you consider seeking those services should you feel the need.

In this chapter, we present some of the likely causes of the strong feelings that you are experiencing and offer you some concrete tips and tools for dealing with them. It is important that you understand that whatever you are feeling is okay and that a range of emotional responses to a high-conflict custody dispute is common and completely understandable.

Common Emotional Responses

Although each high-conflict custody dispute may be unique, there are, of course, common elements, which can set off common emotional responses. One reason you should try to understand and cope with these emotions is that you need to be at your best with your children even when they are being difficult. Some children whose parents are involved in a high-conflict custody dispute can behave disrespectfully, rudely, and hurtfully. Your children may seem completely different from the children you once knew and loved. Your best chance of preserving and protecting your relationship with your children is to have a thick skin, observe appropriate boundaries, and practice a parenting style that communicates unconditional love and a hope for a better future. Managing your emotions is key to achieving your goals.

Fear

It is likely that at some point in your custody dispute, you have felt afraid that your ex's interfering and undermining will result in your losing your children with no hope of recovering them. As bad as things are now, you probably fear they'll get worse. (Note that we are using the term "fear" because we are talking about feelings that are focused on your ex and your custody situation. Worry and anxiety, which are marked by unfocused fear and a more general feeling of unease, are explored later in this chapter.) You also may be afraid of being marginalized and shunned not only by your children but by the community as well. You may be worried that your ex has created a negative image of you, such that your children's teachers and coaches and other people in your community view you as undesirable if not contemptible. Because people are social beings, one of your worst fears may be of feeling alone in the world, denied human connection and meaningful social interaction.

You also might be afraid of your ex. Perhaps your ex has been violent with you in the past, or perhaps he has threatened to be violent or abusive to you. Your ex may have intimidated you or subtly manipulated you throughout the marriage. Your ex's thinly disguised contempt and anger toward you may have become—or you may fear it will become—more direct and intense now that you are divorced. If your ex is seething with rage or is unpredictably emotionally reactive, fear is a normal response to the rational concern that your ex will behave in a frightening or harmful manner toward you.

Unfortunately, in addition to physical harm, there are other things to fear as well. Living with an ex's interfering behavior means living with a tremendous amount of uncertainty about what bad thing might happen next. Each day could be the day your ex files another motion against you in court, harms your relationship with your children, moves away with your children, or turns up somewhere unexpected. Many parents in high-conflict custody disputes have experienced extremely stressful and undeserved negative events—such as being evicted from their home in the middle of the night, coming home to an empty house with the children gone, or being handcuffed and taken away in a police car—due to their ex's strategic maneuvering. Some parents have symptoms of post-traumatic stress disorder (PTSD) based on the intensely frightening experiences they have suffered. Symptoms of PTSD include reliving past traumatic events and being afraid that similar events will occur in the future.

Sometimes it is the not knowing what will happen next that can make you feel afraid. Every time you check your mailbox or your e-mail represents a chance that there could be yet another unpleasant item for you. We know a parent whose heart started racing any time she saw a legal-sized envelope in her mailbox because she thought it meant that her ex was taking her back to court again. Every time you see a car that looks like your ex's car, you may find yourself flinching, thinking that he is nearby. You may think of your ex as your own personal terrorist, plotting to surprise you with yet another intrusion in your life or interference in your relationship with your children.

If you live with constant interference from your ex, it is hard to plan a vacation, a party, or an outing without being afraid that your ex will try to spoil it in some way. Even if she does nothing, the energy you have expended being afraid that she *might* ruin it can be stressful in and of itself. In learning theory, a concept known as "irregular intermittent reinforcement" states that when a certain consequence (in this case a punishment) occurs intermittently (not every time and not in a predictable pattern) in relation to an event, it is very hard to unlearn the association between the event and the consequence. Thus, if your ex disrupts your plans on a periodic basis, you never know during a quiet time when the problem will resurface. You have essentially learned to expect it at random intervals and to feel that it is always lurking in the background, ready to surface at any moment.

Living with this kind of fear can result in physical symptoms of stress, such as headaches, stomachaches, racing heartbeat, difficulty breathing, or full-blown panic attacks. It can also create hypervigilance as you continually scan the environment for any sign of impending threat. Thus, if your ex periodically does not allow the children to be with you during your parenting time, most likely every time you go to pick your children up you will find your stress and tension increasing as you steel yourself for the potential disappointment of being denied your parenting time. Simply knowing that there might be an unpleasant scene could contaminate the joy you feel in anticipation of seeing your children. You will develop a heightened awareness of your surroundings as you are constantly on the lookout for signs of potential intrusion and harm. One parent was keenly aware of the sound of her ex's footsteps, so much so that she could never fully enjoy her daughter's sporting events because she was unconsciously anticipated the sound of his approach. Once he arrived, she knew, he would make things unpleasant for her.

Fear can drain your emotional and physical health. Fear saps the body of much-needed energy. It creates an adrenaline rush, for an "all systems go" situation, as your body gears up for a battle. This is helpful in an actual life-or-death situation, but the body is not made to live in a state of constant fear. When you are on high alert 24/7, the energy you expend protecting yourself from the fear of possible harm is energy that you could have spent doing something more productive; and when you do "come down" from the fear response, you may feel drained and exhausted, as if you just ran a marathon. We should stress that having some or all of these fear reactions is normal and a sign that your nervous system is reacting in a healthy manner to all that is happening to you. In other words, you are supposed to feel such sensations, but you can mitigate the degree to which you feel them.

The first step to help you cope with fear is to determine how realistic your particular fears are. Sometimes when parents are targeted by their ex, they can become afraid and worry about things that are not very likely to happen. It could be helpful for you to take a look at the things that you are afraid of, in order to develop a realistic assessment of the likelihood of their occurrence. Your ex may be taking on a larger-than-life stature in your mind, with the presumed power to cause greater harm than he really can. Even interfering or vindictive ex-spouses are not monsters who are likely to burn your house down or kidnap the children. If you live in constant fear of things that are not likely to happen, you could benefit from knowing that, as it may help alleviate the intensity of your fear response.

In the following exercise, you can make a list of the things that you are most afraid of (e.g., your ex abducting your children, your children moving out, your ex physically harming you) and then indicate how realistic and likely those things actually are. You can also identify ways that you are currently protecting yourself or could protect yourself in the future from the things that you are most afraid of. The more you know and the more you feel protected, the less fearful you will feel. The reason this exercise works is that it "externalizes" the fear you are struggling with, where you can shrink the fear down to size and make it manageable.

It may be helpful to understand that diffuse fear, typically referred to as anxiety, can be self-reinforcing. In other words, the state of vigilance that it creates leads you to find new things to be worried about. It can become a cascading reaction that can eventually lead to the development of a panic disorder. Keep in mind that you have the ability to recognize this cascading and unrealistic state that you may find yourself in and to work toward limiting its effect on you. Recognizing it is the first step to controlling it.

Exercise 2.1: Assessing the Reality of Your Fears

On a piece of paper (e.g., in a journal or notebook), make a list of what you are most afraid of. Then rate the strength of each of your fears on a scale of 1 to 4, where 1 = weak and 4 = very strong. Next, rate each fear as to how realistic you think it is on a scale of 0 to 4, where 0 = not at all realistic, 1 = not very realistic, 2 = somewhat realistic, 3 = mostly realistic, and 4 = highly realistic (if you are unsure, write "unsure"). Finally, indicate next to each fear what you can do to increase your safety and protect yourself from what it is you fear.

Hopefully, this exercise reveals that at least some of the strong fears on your list are not that realistic. You can use this information the next time you become fearful or anxious about those events. Try to remind yourself that those things you very much don't want to happen probably won't. Provide yourself, if you can, with a reality check when you start to have strong fear responses, in order to lower the intensity and spare yourself the unnecessary fear response. For example, you can "reframe" these fears. Instead of "bad things that I think will happen" or "bad things that I am feeling like will happen," think of them as "things I really don't want to happen but probably will not happen." You also might want to take a look at the kinds of things you say to yourself that may be inadvertently increasing your fear. If you find yourself thinking, *I am helpless, I can't survive this*, or *He's going to kill me in court*, you might want to restate your feelings in less extreme and more positive or hopeful ways, such as *I need help getting through this*, *This will be tough, but I know I can handle whatever it is*, or *He may win in court, but I don't know that for sure right now*. You may also want to think about the images you have in your mind. For example, if you see yourself as small and powerless, you might be feeling more afraid than you need to be. Perhaps it would be helpful to remind yourself that you have courage, strength, and resources to help you cope and survive. Picture yourself as competent and strong. Another strategy is to imagine what you would tell a friend who shared her fears with you. Sometimes it is easier for people to handle their emotions when they imagine other people in the same situation.

The best way to deal with a realistic threat is to flee or fight. Therefore, you can try to determine which of the things that you are afraid of you can flee from (i.e., avoid) and which you can fight against. For example, if your ex is threatening to physically harm you, you can avoid being alone with or in close proximity to him. You can request of the court that all transfers of the children take place at a safe, neutral location rather than at one of your homes. If you are worried about your ex abducting your children and you believe that is a rational concern (e.g., he has family abroad and could easily find work in another country), you can petition the court to hold your child's passport. If you are afraid of your friends abandoning you, you can increase your appreciation of them and let them know that if they start to feel drained by your need for support, they can say they need a break and you will not be hurt or angry with them. If you are worried that you will lose your children, you can work on improving your parenting and being mindful of your parenting choices at all times (see Baker and Fine, 2014a, for suggestions).

Another way to help yourself is to create a team of competent and caring legal and mental health professionals to help you navigate your custody dispute. Throughout this book, we will provide you with information and tools you can use to identify, retain, and work with those professionals. Once you have a competent and caring attorney, have a qualified mental health consultant guiding you, and have the best experts on your team, you will hopefully feel less afraid because you will know that you can gain strength and power from these people.

Tips for Calming the Mind, Body, and Spirit

There are a number of mindfulness and relaxation techniques for calming the mind and body after an intense episode of fear and anxiety. Research shows that these exercises often work better than medications (NCCAM 2011).

Deep breathing has been found to be very relaxing, as it empties the mind and slows the heart rate down. In fact, deep breathing exercises are an excellent way to reduce your heart rate (NCCAM 2011). Try breathing in through one nostril and out the other, gently pressing first one nostril shut as you breathe in slowly and then the other as you exhale slowly. Focus only on your breath. If you do this ten times, you will most likely find that your mind and heart have stopped racing. You can continue to breathe in this way for as long as you want to, as often as you want to.

Reciting affirmations of strength can also help you calm down if you find yourself with your heart and mind racing in a frenzy of worry and fear. Try reminding yourself of how strong you are and how much courage you have had to exhibit at various times throughout your life. Reassure yourself that you can handle whatever life throws at you.

Talking to a trusted friend or adviser can also help you regain calmness and clarity when you are distracted by fear and worry. Sometimes you may need to hear the kind voice of a caring friend or therapist or hear validation from someone who knows what it feels like to be going through the same things as you. Make sure that you have people in your life who can "talk you down" through their love and wisdom.

You can also engage in a guided imagery exercise in which you imagine yourself in a beautiful, calm place—the beach, a beautiful meadow, or any place that brings you a sense of inner peace and calmness. Imagine yourself being in that space and feeling that all is right with the world and that you are at one with yourself and nature. Exercises such as these work best when you practice them on a regular basis, because you will get better at them the more you use them.

Although the fear response may be completely understandable and expected in a high-conflict custody dispute, it is essential that you put your strong emotions aside when you are with your children. You need to come across as a competent and capable parent, so "put your game face on." Be calm, positive, and emotionally available to your children, and show them how to be strong and courageous in the face of adversity.

Shame

Imagine that someone you have just met asks you a question about your ex or your children. If your children are currently very angry with and rejecting of you, most likely even an innocuous question would be quite painful for you and pose a dilemma. On one hand, you could answer as if everything were normal in your relationship with your children, although that could make you feel as if you were lying. On the other hand, you could be honest and reveal the terrible truth that you live with every day, which is perhaps that your children haven't spoken to you in weeks or even months and you really don't know what they are doing for the summer, how they like their new soccer coach, or which colleges they plan to apply to. You might also feel ashamed that you are in constant conflict with your ex, as if that says something about what kind of person you are.

In addition to all the other emotions you might feel in such a situation (and confusion as to how to respond), you might experience some element of shame. Perhaps your new acquaintance would respond in horror if you said that your children do not live with you or do not speak with you, for example, leading you to feel ashamed. But most likely you already carry around that feeling of shame anyway. The basis of this shame, at least in part, is the feeling that you have done something to deserve your children's (and your ex's) animosity or that there is something inherent in you that warrants rejection.

The reason parents whose children have rejected them in response to a high-conflict custody dispute are so ready to believe that they have caused or deserve their children's rejection is that, since all parents are imperfect, there is often a grain of truth to their children's complaints and their ex's accusations. Most likely, on some level, you understand that the negative things your children say about you are usually very big distortions of very small truths. Your ex has taken your imperfections (which all parents have) and created a lie built on that fact. To your children, the lie feels like a truth (especially since it is most likely often repeated by your ex). For example, your ex tells the children that you abandoned them, because you are the one who moved out of the house after the separation. What your ex doesn't tell the children, however, is that it was a joint decision based on a rational appraisal of what would be easiest for the children (or perhaps your ex threatened you so that you had to move out). All your children know is that you left them, and they will—based on their own experience—believe it when your ex tells them that "[Mommy/Daddy] left us." Or perhaps you are a bit of an early bird, showing up a few minutes early for any appointment. Your children probably experienced you rushing them to get ready for various events over the course of their life. So when your ex tells them that you are always rushing them because you are inconsiderate or because you have a mental illness, it might ring true to them because they remember you often rushing them. The same thing applies to conflict with your ex. There could be a grain of truth to her complaints about you, but that doesn't mean that you deserve the level of animosity she displays toward you. For example, perhaps you did hang up on her when she called you the other day, but it was in response to her berating and cursing at you. It can be difficult to keep cause and effect straight, especially when your ex is working double time to convince everyone that your (minor) flaws are the true cause of the conflict you are experiencing with her and the children.

There is an old saying that if ten people tell you you're drunk, you probably should sit down (meaning that you are in fact drunk).

Any person with even a modicum of introspective ability and humility is likely to say to himself, *If everyone is telling me I am [bossy/mean/timid/inconsiderate], I probably really am that way.* Thus, you are likely to have doubts about the extent to which you are not the cause of your children's rejection, because so many people seem to believe that you are. You may understand intellectually that your children's rejection of you is unjustifiable, but feel otherwise in your heart. You may find yourself reviewing your faults and flaws and berating yourself for not having done better. This can result in your feeling responsible for the rejection and thus makes you susceptible to the implied blame and shame that others (your ex, the children, the evaluator, the judge, etc.) cast on you. You also may have a personal tendency toward a shame-based response to many situations, not just the current conflict with your children and/or ex. If so, it could be helpful to explore this in individual therapy.

In coping with shame, first, it is essential that you understand that most children would not reject a parent, especially for the types of minor parenting flaws that you have probably exhibited. You need to be very clear in your own mind about the difference between normal parenting (in all its variations) and the kinds of parenting behaviors that would result in a child's rejecting a parent. Perhaps it would help to consult with an expert on child abuse in order to learn about how even the most horribly abused child usually wants to maintain a relationship with his abusive parents. You could also think about how you probably forgave your own parents for most of their parenting flaws. Also consider your ex's parenting flaws and how willing your children are to give *him* a free pass for his limitations. Most likely, your children are much harder on you for much less severe deficits than they are on your ex. This should tell you that your children are not responding in a rational way to your actual behavior. It also might help to remind yourself that some degree of parent-child conflict and children's testing of parents' limits is normative, especially in divorced families, in which children can play the parents off each other.

Exercise 2.2: Assessing the Sources of Your Shame

On a piece of paper (e.g., in a journal or notebook), make a list of the ten worst things you have ever done to your children. For example, perhaps you have been late picking them up from school or yelled at them to stop texting your ex when you were trying to spend time with them. Perhaps you picked up your toddler in anger and placed her in a time-out in a way that didn't feel good for her. Next, objectively rate how harmful each of these was on a scale of 0 to 4, where 0 = not at all harmful and 4 = very harmful. Ask yourself whether these are truly the kinds of parenting behaviors that would result in a child's never wanting to speak to a parent again. Next, indicate whether you have or need to apologize to your children for your actions.

Hopefully, this will help you develop an understanding that nothing you have done would result in your children's rejection of you were it not for your ex fanning the flames of their discontent and encouraging if not pressuring them to be hurt and angry with you. At the same time, if you have done things for which you owe your children an apology, consider apologizing (although check with your attorney first about how to do that, as it could affect your legal case).

(A word of caution is necessary here. As you work through these exercises, make certain to keep your notes in a secure location—one that is not accessible to your children. Such documents could be distorted and presented to the court as evidence of your wrongdoing. Change all of your computer and online passwords, secure all hard and flash drives, and put a screen lock on your computer.)

Try to remember that the range of parenting styles, attitudes, and attributes that are considered acceptable is broad. Even with overly permissive or overly restrictive parents, children can still grow up fully normal and with a firm foundation. Having done the preceding exercise, you might decide that despite your parenting being appropriate and capable, you want to modify some of your parenting choices and decisions so as to create a more harmonious relationship between you and your children. In other words, in light of your custody dispute, some accommodations in your parenting may be warranted. If so, you need not feel ashamed. Realizing that changes would be helpful does not mean you have been a bad parent.

It also might be helpful to take a look at the things that you say to yourself about your parenting situation. For example, if you think, *I am such a failure!* and *Nothing I do turns out right*, try to gently steer your mind to more charitable thoughts, such as *I am not a perfect parent, but I have done a lot of good for my children*. Also, you can ask yourself how your parenting choices look when you imagine they were made by someone else. Do the things that seem so terrible when you think about *you* doing them seem less bad when you imagine someone else doing them?

Tips for Coping with Shame

Shame is an uncomfortable and often unnecessary experience. Here are some things you can do to limit and manage your shameful feelings.

○ Avoid situations that you know will be particularly shaming, unless you absolutely must participate.

○ If you choose to attend an event that is likely to create a feeling of shame for you, remind yourself that you are a good and loving parent and that you do not deserve poor treatment by your children or your ex.

○ Anticipate how you want to respond to questions that are likely to arise so that you are not caught off guard. Give yourself permission to tell white lies to strangers should they ask about your children. "They're fine—how are yours?" is okay to say to someone at a party. You are not obligated to share your personal story with everyone who happens to ask you how you are doing.

Understand that your shame response is actually your own distortion of who you are. Once you clearly understand and "own" this truth, you can view these uncomfortable situations as opportunities to overcome the distortion. The best way to overcome an irrational fear is to gradually expose yourself to what it is you fear and in this way learn through personal experience that it is not so dangerous. The way to conquer a phobia of bridges, for example, is to eventually go over a bridge. In this way, your fear of these situations can provide you with the opportunity to work through your feelings.

Shame can make you want to hide and withdraw in order to avoid negative judgment by others. However, during your parenting time, you do not have the luxury of running away. You must "step up to the plate" and be a loving, present, and involved parent to your children despite any feelings of insecurity and shame. Otherwise, you will be confirming for your children that you are unworthy of their love or that your emotional problems are preventing you from being a healthy presence in their lives.

Loneliness

Many parents in high-conflict custody disputes would say that their friends and family (as well as their neighbors, bosses, and coworkers, among others) blame them for their plight or in some way significantly misunderstand their experience. Perhaps your friends are telling you to stop being a worrywart or to stop obsessing about what your ex is going to do next. Perhaps your coworker insensitively goes on and on about how much fun she had with her children the past weekend despite knowing that you were once again denied your parenting time. Perhaps your family has implied that the situation is your fault because you married your ex, you signed a bad agreement, you chose a bad attorney, or you allowed your ex to walk all over you. Perhaps your friends tell you to stop chasing after your children and to let them come around when they are ready, or perhaps they minimize your concerns about the harm being done to your children, telling you that your children are making their own choices and must live with the consequences.

There are a lot of ill-informed people in the world who do not understand what you are going through and think that anybody who is in a high-conflict custody dispute must have done something to deserve it. People don't like to think of the world as an unjust place in which good parents lose their children to evil exes who brainwashed the children and were aided by ill-informed and dysfunctional family courts. They might assume that you are paranoid or overly defensive when you try to explain what is going on. For all of these reasons, you may feel that virtually no one in your close circle understands what you are going through. Feelings of loneliness and isolation are common by-products of being misunderstood in this way.

Such feelings of being lonely tend to grow if left unattended. If you cannot share your trials and tribulations and worries with someone who can show concern for you and validate your experience, you may feel isolated. This is the last thing that you need at a time of extreme stress. The loving support of friends and family members can be very helpful. In coping with loneliness, it will be very important for you to identify people in your circle of acquaintances who you feel understand what you are going through.

Exercise 2.3: Assessing Your Social Support Network

On the left side of a piece of paper (e.g., in a journal or notebook), write down the name of each person in your social support network (e.g., your mother, father, sister, brother, boss, coworker, neighbor, community or religious leader). Then rate how well each person, in your opinion, currently understands and supports you in your custody dispute on a scale of 0 to 4, where 0 = not at all and 4 = very well. Bear in mind that someone might be very helpful and supportive in other areas of your life but not with your custody dispute, and vice versa.

If some people currently do not "get it" but you believe they may in the future, think about what you can do to bring them around and enhance their supportiveness. Examples are having a frank discussion with them about feeling alone and misunderstood and giving them a book to read about high-conflict custody disputes—and perhaps a book on parental alienation, such as *Adult Children of Parental Alienation Syndrome: Breaking the Ties That Bind*, by Amy Baker (2007), or *Surviving Parental Alienation: A Journey of Hope and Healing*, by Amy Baker and Paul Fine (2014b)—to bring them up to speed on your issues. Another idea is to bring them to a support group for parents in your situation (with the permission of the support group leader) to introduce them to other people who are dealing with similar situations. Write down some ways like these you can help particular people in your social support network be more understanding and supportive of your custody dispute.

If there are people who do not currently understand your situation and you do not feel that you can bring them around, you can choose to avoid discussing your custody dispute with those people in the future. You can still relate to them about other things (perhaps). Think of this as choosing to not look for water in a well that is dry. You are not going to get what you need out of that interaction.

For people who you feel are currently supportive, remember to show your appreciation and gratitude for their help. Also, make sure to ask them how *they* are doing so that you don't lose sight of whatever is going on in *their* lives. You can also invite them to let you know if they have heard about your custody dispute one too many times and need a break. Let them know that you understand that it can be hard to bear witness to your pain and that you appreciate how much they have already been there for you. It may not always be fun or easy for them to hear what you are going through. Be aware of "empathy fatigue" on the part of friends and family members who may have heard your tale of woe on an ongoing basis for years.

Once you identify action steps, you will hopefully feel more empowered.

> ## Tips for Coping with Feeling Alone
>
> It can be hard to feel as if you are facing a problem alone. Following are some suggestions for breaking through the isolation.
>
> - Join an online or face-to-face support group for parents going through a high-conflict custody dispute.
>
> - Read stories written about custody disputes by other parents like you, such as those in *Surviving Parental Alienation: A Journey of Hope and Healing* (Baker and Fine 2014b). (Keep in mind, however, that stories about worse situations than yours or with particularly bleak and negative outcomes can be frightening.)
>
> - Write up your experience in a story, poem, or song, and share it with others.
>
> - Remind yourself that not everyone will understand your situation. It is complicated and sometimes goes against beliefs and assumptions that most people hold about how the world works, how children behave, and how families function.
>
> - Seek professional counseling from a mental health professional who you are confident is familiar with the issues involved in high-conflict custody disputes.

Sadness

Many parents dealing with a high-conflict custody dispute, especially when they believe that their ex is undermining and interfering in their relationship with their children, have moments or periods of sadness. This is a common and normal emotional response to a very difficult experience. There are many reasons you might experience sadness at some point along the way. First, being the object of your ex's rage and aggression (whether overt or covert) doesn't feel good. It can be quite unpleasant to have someone be so angry at you that she wants to hurt you (and your children). It is probably hard not to feel sad at the sorry state of your divorce (and probably your marriage), in which your ex is involving the children in your conflict and trying to interfere with your relationship with them. No one wants to have an ugly divorce and custody battle. Most people probably think they will have an amicable or at least manageable divorce. Any time people's hopes, dreams, plans, and expectations are not realized, they may feel sadness at the direction their life has taken.

You might also feel sadness when you miss out on opportunities to spend time with your children; and the more you miss out, the sadder you might become. Do not expect that you will get used to not having your children in your life. Most likely, every day that goes by without contact with your children will make you yearn for them. Obviously, you might feel even sadder than usual on special events when you would have a reasonable expectation of being with your children. This would include milestones in your life (e.g., your birthday), milestones in your children's lives (e.g., their birthdays, graduations, learning to drive), holidays, vacations, and extracurricular events. Most likely, there are at least one or two of these important days each month that you miss spending with your children. These could be particularly difficult days for you.

These times can be especially difficult if—in addition to experiencing your own pain and sadness—you also witness and experience members of your family feeling hurt and disappointed by the conflict between you and your ex, especially if it involves the loss of your children. Some targeted parents have parents who once had close and loving relationships with their grandchildren, only to suddenly be banished from their lives. These parents may be confused, hurt, and angry at the situation. If your parents are ill or elderly, it can be particularly painful for both you and them, as you are most likely aware of the limited time left for them to have a relationship with your children. This adds another layer to the sadness in your life. Likewise, if your parents once had a close and loving relationship with your ex, they may feel bewildered at the level of animosity he displays toward them and feel tremendous loss and sadness.

Another cause for sadness is when you acknowledge the ways in which your children have been harmed, warped, corrupted, or otherwise negatively affected by the custody dispute. If you have information about how your children are doing when they are not with you, you may have the unpleasant experience of knowing that their personality and moral character are being affected by your ex's actions and attitudes. Some children whose parents are in a custody dispute become overly empowered and entitled, and this can lead them to behave in a rude and arrogant manner. It is hard to see one's children behave in such an unwholesome way, knowing that it will likely cause them problems later in life in terms of managing interpersonal relationships on the job and in their personal life. Some children forgo formerly beloved hobbies and interests and talents just to please a parent, and perhaps this is true of your children. Perhaps you have seen their grades slip. Perhaps your children have engaged in risky behaviors, such as experimenting with drugs or alcohol. While proclaiming to have their children's best interests at heart, many parents—and your ex may be one of them—do not, and it must be extremely painful to watch your beloved children be subjected to the negative influence of your ex, especially when you are not able to provide a corrective influence for them.

Sadness can be hard to contain to just one area of your life. It can take on a life of its own, permeating all areas of your life, tingeing even the best of experiences with a sense of darkness and hopelessness. In coping with sadness, it is very important to keep tabs on your mood to determine how pervasive your sadness is. If you have concerns that your sadness has evolved into depression (a pervasive feeling of hopelessness and despair), contact a licensed mental health professional. The following exercise can help you assess whether your sadness has become depression. Please note that this is not a formal depression inventory but a guide to help you organize your thoughts about your feelings and symptoms.

Exercise 2.4: Assessing Depression

Number a piece of paper (e.g., in a journal or notebook) from 1 to 8. Then, answer the questions below using the following key:

0 = Never

1 = Rarely

2 = Sometimes

3 = Often

4 = Very Often

How often in the past two weeks have you...

1. experienced a lack of pleasure in everyday activities?

2. had less energy than usual?

3. felt tired and lethargic?

4. had difficulty falling asleep or staying asleep?

5. noticed unintended changes in eating or weight?

6. felt like a failure?

7. felt hopeless?

8. had thoughts about harming yourself?

This is not a screening test, so there is no need to add up your scores. The purpose of this exercise is only to help you realize that depression may manifest in many different ways, not just as a feeling of sadness. Perhaps you are experiencing several of these symptoms often. If so, whether or not you pursue evaluation by a medical or mental health professional, it may help to try some of the suggestions for alleviating sadness in the remainder of this section.

Whether you are experiencing sadness or depression, take care of yourself and do what you can to brighten your mood and lift your spirits. Although is it not likely that you can be completely free of sadness as long as you are in a high-conflict custody dispute, you do not need to suffer from it excessively.

Our first suggestion for coping with sadness is to engage in an act of kindness toward another person. Psychiatrist Alfred Adler is said to have encouraged a depressed client to do something nice for someone else. When the client explained that he was really quite depressed, Adler assigned him the task of doing two nice things. Adler understood that one way to battle depression and sadness is to get outside of ourselves and be a positive force in the world. Doing so may not directly improve your situation, but it can improve your outlook. It probably doesn't matter what you do, as long as you do it with warmth and kindness. You may be surprised at how much your mood lifts when you do something nice for someone else. However, we do advise that you stay away from efforts to change legislation in the family courts, as that could rankle the judge and result in the perception that you are obsessed. Instead, do charity or volunteer work to benefit others.

Sometimes people feel sad because they feel that nothing will ever get better—that is, they have a feeling of hopelessness. If this is true of you, you may be able to reduce your sadness by making sure that you have a realistic assessment of the hopefulness of your situation. There may be aspects that are in fact hopeless—your ex, for example, might not ever change his desire to punish you or control your children)—but other aspects may not be as hopeless as they feel. For example, it might be helpful to remind yourself that some children caught in a loyalty conflict come around and reconnect with a parent with whom they were once very angry. Perhaps reading such stories as those in *Adult Children of Parental Alienation Syndrome* by Amy Baker (2007) or *Surviving Parental Alienation* by Amy Baker and Paul Fine (2014b) can help you remember that there is no point or need to assume that your children will remain angry and hurt with you forever. It will probably help to "take the long view" about your situation. That means keeping your eye on your long-term goal, which is to have a relationship with your children for the rest of your life. Hiring a team of legal and mental health professionals, taking care of yourself emotionally, and reaching out to your children to let them know that you love them and want a relationship with them will increase the likelihood that you'll achieve your goal of resolving the conflict. You may need to stop every once in a while and take stock of all the ways you are working toward your goal, and you may need to remind yourself of whatever successes you have achieved on the legal front or with respect to your relationship with your children.

Another way to battle sadness is to develop a deep sense of gratitude for what *is* good and right in your life. It is often easy to become consumed by the custody dispute drama and trauma. If you find that this is happening to you, you might benefit from a reminder that not everything in your life involves sadness and suffering. There is no benefit to suffering endlessly, and there is no need for you to feel guilty for having some pleasure in your life. If you can and do experience some pleasure, it can actually help strengthen you for the battles that lie ahead.

Tips for Developing Gratitude

You may be so focused on your struggle that you often forget to notice and be grateful for the parts of your life that are working well. Now is the time to take stock and feel appreciative of the good.

○ Make a list of ten things that you are grateful for. Post the list where you are likely to see it often, and take a moment each day to reflect on those things. Research has shown that naming and writing down three things per day that you are grateful for or appreciative of can have a powerful effect on even severe depression within a very short period of time (Harvard Mental Health Newsletter 2011). But you must do it to benefit from it.

○ Say a blessing of thanks before each meal or at bedtime. Make a ritual of being thankful for what you have in your life.

○ Volunteer at a homeless shelter or an animal shelter in order to remember others' suffering. As bad as you have it, there are always others who have it worse. It cannot hurt to periodically remember that there are many ways to suffer in this life and being in a high-conflict custody dispute is but one way.

○ Develop a gratitude mantra, such as a short saying or poem that reflects what gratitude means to you and what you are grateful for.

You can also counter sadness by being aware of your thoughts. People who engage in certain types of thinking are more likely to experience depression, so it is helpful to know what kinds of thoughts to try to avoid. The three types of thoughts most likely to lead to depression are:

1. Thoughts that blame you for all the bad things in your life, such as *I can't do anything right* or *I am such a loser*

2. Thoughts that focus on the permanence of the bad things that happen, such as *Nothing will ever get better* and *It's hopeless*

3. Thoughts that spread bad feelings about one area of your life (e.g., your custody dispute) to other areas so that instead of thinking that a particular event is bad or difficult you say to yourself, *Everything is really hard* or *Nothing is going right*

Try to be aware of those types of thoughts and remind yourself that most likely they are not true. It might help to actively counter them by focusing on the facts that (1) not everything is *your* fault, (2) the bad times and sad feelings will *not* last forever, and (3) not *everything* in your life is terrible and painful.

As previously noted, strong feelings are understandable when you are in a high-conflict custody dispute. However, you must do everything possible to not let those strong feelings permeate your interactions and relationship with your children. To give into the depression or sadness to such an extent that it corrupts your relationship with your children will confirm the negative messages they are hearing about you. If you are too sad to enjoy their company, they will believe that you truly don't love them. Therefore, you must model courage and positive attitudes as a parent so as to instill those important values in them and to reassure them that your love for them is stronger than the disagreements you have with their other parent.

Anger

It is also natural to feel anger when you are in a custody dispute, and there certainly is plenty to feel angry about. You may feel angry at your ex for betraying your relationship and the sacred trust you thought you shared in taking care of and nurturing your children. There must have been a time when you trusted this person and believed that you and he would have a mutually supportive bond for the rest of your lives. To now be faced with that person's lies and deceptions and nasty tactics can be enraging. If your ex has stolen money from you, has had you wrongly arrested, has made a false abuse or domestic violence charge against you, has had you fired, has stolen your property, or has engaged in any other illegal and/or underhanded behavior that greatly inconvenienced you, you are also likely quite angry about that.

You may also feel anger at your ex for hurting your children by interfering in your relationship with them and by encouraging them to behave in a rude and entitled manner. It is very painful to see your children take on your ex's negative attitudes, and you may rightly feel angry at your ex for working so hard to prevent your children from being their best selves.

You also might be angry at the legal and mental health professionals who have so far let you down. This might include uncaring or incompetent attorneys who gave you bad advice or did not effectively protect your rights or advocate on your behalf. You might feel angry at the judge or the custody evaluator if he did not seem to care enough to understand what was really going on in your family.

Certainly, if you paid considerable amounts of money to your attorney and the evaluator and you did not feel listened to or cared about, you have a right to feel exploited and angry. Many such parents focus their anger on what they perceive to be an overburdened and uncaring family court system. Because family court judges have a wide degree of judicial discretion, it is hard not to blame the judge when a decision goes against you (especially when the facts and evidence were in your favor). Many parents feel that cronyism is common in family court, particularly in some jurisdictions, and to the extent that this is the case, one might rightly feel quite angry about that. A pervasive feeling of being the victim of an injustice can also result in chronic anger at "the system" for failing you and your children.

Anger would also be a natural response to therapists and reunification specialists who did nothing more than enable your ex to continue to manipulate and control your children, choosing to take a "wait and see" approach or claiming that your children "are not ready" to have a relationship with you. You may even have been encouraged to apologize to your children for things you did not do. Therapists who endorse the "hybrid" model—a belief that most high-conflict custody disputes reflect deficits on the part of both parents and that when children reject a parent it is usually warranted—can also incite anger, because the therapist will be focusing his attention on your apparent flaws as a significant cause of your children's rejection. You might also feel anger at a mediator or attorney who encouraged you to compromise with your ex despite the fact that you had already made considerable concessions to her. You might easily be angered at the thought of your time and money that was wasted.

Although the anger you experience as a result of your custody dispute is mostly if not entirely justified, it is not entirely helpful to you. Some anger is a good thing, as it is a signal to your mind and body that something is not right. The anger may be telling you to get a new attorney or to work harder to make your case to the judge, or it could compel you to dig deeper in your efforts at self-improvement. It may be telling you that you need to enhance your legal team so that you have the best chance of making your case to the judge. Anger can create energy and motivation to right a wrong, and in that sense it can be a powerful tool.

However, living with a steady stream of anger coursing through you can be quite draining mentally and physically. Chronic anger can cause ulcers, high blood pressure, and digestive problems. If you let your anger at your ex or the "system" permeate your life, it can strain your relationships with others (e.g., your significant other, your coworkers, your friends, your neighbors). Anger can also lead you to rash action that can harm your case and your cause. Thus, if you ever sit down to write an e-mail to your attorney, the custody evaluator, or your ex while you are in a state of agitation, do not hit the "send" button. Never send an important communication while angry. You can use the anger to fuel your desire to communicate, but do not actually complete the communication process while angry. Save the draft, and read it again later with a cooler head. Show the e-mail to a friend, your attorney, or a coach to get some objective feedback about whether it will help or hurt your situation.

Likewise, trying to solve a problem while angry makes it likely that you will not consider all your options. Although anger creates energy and a feeling of wanting to act right this very minute, it also constricts your thinking such that you become overly focused on the solution most likely to allow you to discharge your anger. That solution might not actually be the best one for you. Try to see whether you can slow down the process in order to engage in a more rational problem-solving approach, one that involves sitting down (alone, with a friend, or with a mental health professional) and clearly articulating the problem. Sometimes when you do this, you will realize that you are not really angry about the thing you thought you were angry about; something else is bothering you. Once you identify the source(s) of your anger, brainstorm every conceivable solution. Don't rule anything out at this point, because even a wild idea could lead you to come up with a good solution. You may end up deciding that your original impulse is the right solution, but you will have done no harm by taking a more thoughtful approach.

Sometimes when people are angry, they engage in thinking that exacerbates and inflames the anger. Take a look at the thoughts running through your head while you are feeling angry, to see whether that is happening with you. Are you having thoughts like *This is a disaster! I have never seen such incompetence!* or *I have the worst attorney in the world! She never listens to me!* If you are using extreme words such as "always" and "never," most likely you are catastrophizing, or making things seem worse than they are. Catastrophizing can make you feel worse, can cloud your judgment, and can spur you to take actions that you will regret. Be aware of times when you are angry, and make sure that your actions are ones that you will be proud of tomorrow, when the anger subsides.

Tips for Coping with Anger

When you find that anger is controlling you, here are some things to try so that you can regain your control.

○ Notice how the anger feels in your body. Is your heart racing? Are your fists clenched? Are you breathing rapidly? Where do you feel the anger? Just noticing your body can help you calm down and regain control.

○ Engage in some kind of meditation practice, such as breathing deeply, to cleanse your mind and body of the anger. Meditation and deep breathing can calm your mind and body and allow you to release some of the anger that is bottled up inside of you.

○ Develop a mantra (a saying) that helps calm you down. Use positive self-talk and such as "I can handle this" and "This will pass," to remind yourself that you are strong and can handle whatever the situation is.

It might be helpful to remember that you haven't been singled out for your terrible fate of having a hostile ex and a high-conflict custody dispute. Bad things happen to all sorts of people, and injustice is unfortunately part of the way the world works, with all its imperfections. Knowing that the universe hasn't singled you out can hopefully help alleviate some of the angry feelings.

Despite feeling angry at your ex or even at your children for their provocative behavior, you must try hard to control your strong emotional responses and interact in a calm and loving manner with your children at all times. Likewise, you should avoid dramatic displays of anger toward your ex, because they will most likely inflame your relationship with him. Develop tools for controlling your anger so that you are always behaving in an appropriate manner.

Worry

Some people are natural worriers. Their minds tend to go right to the place of uncertainty, the way a child's tongue goes to the place where a baby tooth just came out. It feels like a natural thing to do, to mull over a problem and consider the "what ifs."

As a parent involved in a high-conflict custody dispute, you probably have a lot to worry about. You may be worried about your legal case. You may wonder whether you have the right or the best attorney for you. Unless you are a family attorney yourself, a lot of what goes on in court and in legal preparations is going to be unfamiliar to you. You have no way of knowing whether a particular motion was well done (outside the obvious absence of typos and factual mistakes). You can't know whether your legal strategy will be effective or is even appropriate. You are basically at the mercy of your attorney. The stakes are extremely high, and you don't have much by way of feedback to judge whether you are on the right course.

You might also worry about your finances in light of the expensive nature of high-conflict custody disputes. Many parents note how the expenses keep increasing long before any results are evident in court. Once you have retained consultants, experts, and evaluators, the expenses will increase even further. Some fortunate people can take a "spare no expense" approach to their custody dispute, but many people—even those who most would consider wealthy— worry about the mounting costs. Every penny spent on their legal case is money that could have been spent on retirement or the children's college tuition.

Some parents worry about how they will fare under the pressure of a deposition or cross-examination. Most likely, you have never been a witness in a case before and have never testified under oath. However, you have probably seen on television a naïve witness being reduced to tears and humiliation under the withering attack of an aggressive attorney. It is the rare person indeed who would look forward to sparring with an attorney on the stand, especially when the stakes are so high. This might cast an increasingly large shadow over you as a court date looms.

You may also worry about whether your friends and family will be able to continue to support and assist you. If you rely extensively on friends, family, neighbors, or coworkers for things like babysitting, money, or emotional support during your custody dispute, you may worry that their goodwill and/or patience will wear out.

You might also be worried that as bad as things are with your ex or with your children, they could become worse. If you currently have contact with your children, they could decide to cut you off, or your ex could stop allowing them to spend any time with you. If your children usually have difficulty transitioning to your home but then eventually settle in and relate nicely with you, that could change— your children might start to hole up in their bedrooms and wait out your parenting time. You might worry that you will make a parenting mistake that could turn out to be "the one" that results in their cutting you off completely. If you have an ex who seems to make it his second career to destroy or inconvenience you, you are likely worried about what his next move will be. Because you don't really have any control over your ex and his negative influence on your children, it is easy to worry about what might happen next.

You may also worry that you will run out of steam and be unable to forge ahead in your battle to save your relationship with your children. You may worry that you will run out of time, money, energy, or good advice and simply have to stop pursuing a legal remedy altogether.

As with other emotions, there is a positive side to worrying. It is a signal that something doesn't feel right. It directs the mind to pay attention to something, with the possibility that through extensive thinking about and mulling over a problem, you can arrive at a solution. Sometimes, worry can indeed help you solve problems.

On the downside, extensive worrying can drain you mentally and physically. It can keep you up at night, preventing you from getting a good night's sleep and feeling rested the next day. Worry can create anxiety, as it focuses you on the "what ifs" and all the bad things that could happen. Worry is really the cognitive expression of anxiety, such that worry feeds anxiety and anxiety feeds worry. Worrying can also be a distraction and make it difficult for you to concentrate. Do you ever find yourself at work or playing with the children and you realize that you haven't been paying attention to what you were doing because your mind has gone back to the same old problem once again? It's like a mental rut that you can't get out of that takes you away from the task or the pleasure at hand. You certainly do not want your worries about your custody dispute to take you away from enjoying the time that you do have with your children.

Excessive worrying can also create paralysis: your mind stays focused on the problem and not on identifying workable solutions. You may find something to worry about with respect to each solution and thus be unable to move past the worrying phase. There are times when you must act decisively, and it would not be helpful if you were stuck worrying and unable to make decisions when needed. There are definite timelines and deadlines in family court, and you must be able to function within them.

The following exercise will help you identify the cause of your worries and determine whether your level and style of worrying is helping or hurting you.

Exercise 2.5: What Is Worrying You

On a piece of paper (e.g., in a journal or notebook), make a list of all the things that are worrying you about your custody dispute and your relationship with your ex and your children. Next to each item, indicate how often you worry about it on a scale of 1 to 4, where 1 = rarely and 4 = very often. Is the worrying helping you identify solutions? If so, write "helpful." If the worrying is not helping you identify solutions or is preventing you from achieving your goals, write "not helpful."

If you believe that your worrying is hurting more than helping, we encourage you to try a new way of worrying, outlined below, to see whether it can help you solve problems more efficiently.

First, when you notice that you are worrying, write down what is worrying you. That way, you are honoring the topic and giving it a place to be while you focus on other things. You don't want to stop yourself from thinking about the problem; you just want to think about it at a time and place that works for you. You might even try saying out loud, "This is a problem I will think over when the time is right," to reassure yourself that you will address it.

Second, create a time and place every day to look over your list of worries and consider how to handle them. By predetermining a time and a place, you are limiting the amount of time that you will allocate to worrying. When you acclimate yourself to doing your worrying at a specified time and place, you are training your mind to let go of worries during the rest of the day.

Third, make a note of each worry and decide whether the problem behind it is solvable or not. Some problems simply cannot be solved, and there is no point in worrying about them. You might need to remind yourself (you can use the Serenity Prayer) that some things are out of your control. Perhaps there is a way you can take a worry about an unsolvable problem and turn it into a solvable problem. For example, you don't need to worry endlessly that your ex will take you back to court. You have no control over that and have no way of knowing what his plans are. But you could constructively focus on what you would do *if* that happened and prepare now for that eventuality. That could involve interviewing and retaining attorneys, finding a mental health consultant, setting aside money, and preparing your evidence. In that way, should you receive notice that a motion has been filed against you, you will be mentally and emotionally prepared. Likewise, you have no control over your ex's personality and should relieve yourself of the need to worry about his narcissism, his borderline personality disorder, or whatever you think his problem is. But you could benefit from reading about narcissism, borderline personality disorder, or whatever disorder you think he has and thinking about ways you could alter your behavior to improve your relationship with him based on what you learn.

Since worrying is a habit in thinking, it is important to understand that, like any habit, it can be modified or unlearned. The important thing to remember is that if you simply give in to the habit of excessive worrying, it will most likely increase and become more debilitating. The suggestions above are actually tools that put your thoughts more under your conscious control. With practice, you can regain control over your runaway thoughts. Below are some additional tips to help you when you find yourself caught up in a storm of worry.

Tips for Coping with Worrying

Be aware of any thinking that inflames the worrying, such as catastrophizing—for example, *It would be the worst thing in the world if....*

Remind yourself that you are strong and can handle any adversity. You might not like it, but you can cope with it.

Learn to embrace uncertainty. Understand and accept that no one can know what will happen next and that being alive involves living each moment as it comes. Worry cannot provide you with the control you may seek.

Like worry, any negative emotional response discussed in this chapter can become mentally ingrained, a "rut in the road." When anger, sadness, fear, shame, or loneliness becomes your automatic reaction to a variety of situations, it can be problematic. For this reason, awareness of your emotional responses and habits will be helpful throughout your life.

Conclusion

As a parent in a high-conflict custody dispute, you may experience a range of negative and unpleasant emotions over the course of any particular day. You may feel afraid, ashamed, alone, sad, angry, and worried. All of these emotions are completely understandable and okay. You may also experience other emotions as well, such as frustration and guilt. This is to be expected, because having an undermining and interfering ex causes a great deal of intrusion and disrupts your ability to live your life the way you want. Each of these emotions can be helpful as a signal to you that something needs to change; however, each one—if excessive—can also drain you of energy, spirit, and the ability to enjoy your life. We encourage you to keep an eye on your emotional life and take the time to develop enhanced coping skills so that you will have the inner resources you need to live your life despite being in a high-conflict custody dispute.

CHAPTER 3

Finding and Working
with the Right Attorney

Rather than being self-represented (known as being pro se or pro per), many parents in high-conflict custody disputes retain an attorney to represent them in family court. (Retaining an attorney means paying him a lump sum up front, which he will charge his work against. It also involves signing a contract.) If you do not have an attorney at the moment, you may eventually want or need one, and it is better to start looking sooner rather than later. If you already have an attorney, you may still want to read this chapter, because many parents change attorneys at least once over the course of their custody dispute, and it helps to know what you should look for.

The purpose of this chapter is to help you avoid feeling unnecessarily hurt by, confused about, angry with, or disappointed in the person you choose to represent you in your legal actions. We know from research that many parents in custody disputes feel high levels of dissatisfaction with their attorneys (Baker 2010). They report that the attorney is not caring and compassionate toward them, is not competent in addressing their issues, does not advocate for their rights, does not communicate with them on a timely basis, or has failed to advise them on and prepare them for various aspects of their case. This is certainly disheartening news, but you can learn from these parents' experience.

One way to do that is to be clear in your own mind about what your attorney is able and willing to do for you. Your attorney is not your friend, your confidante, your source of emotional support, or your mental health provider. She is not necessarily going to explain the ins and outs of a custody evaluation or what to expect in a psychological evaluation (although ideally she will). You will be spared anger and disappointment if you do not look for or ask for something from your attorney that is outside her role and skill set and possibly outside her comfort zone. Your attorney's job is to be familiar with the relevant laws, understand how to apply them in your case, explain your options and the likely outcomes of those options to you, prepare the necessary documents in a timely manner that allows you time to provide thoughtful feedback, and oversee the legal strategy (including going to court if necessary) to help you achieve your goals. Even just focusing on what your attorney *is* supposed to do, you can see that hiring the right attorney is the single most important decision you will make with respect to your custody dispute.

Finding the Right Attorney

The best time to find a good attorney is *before* you are facing a legal emergency so that you will not have to "shop around" for one under the pressure of an impending deadline. Even if you have just been served with papers or found out that your ex has taken some action that you feel you need to immediately respond to in a legal venue—whether it be enrolling your children in a new school without your approval or deciding to move with the children to another state—and you feel desperate, it is important to be thoughtful and selective when choosing and retaining an attorney. The consequences of this choice could reverberate in your life for years to come.

Referral Sources

Whether you are in immediate need of legal advice and services or not, it is time to make a list of potential attorneys. Obviously, if you know someone who has worked with an attorney and achieved good outcomes when dealing with a similar situation—for example, an ex who wanted to move away with the children or was limiting contact and communication with the children—you will want to start by getting that attorney's name. Many communities have support networks for parents in high-conflict custody disputes, such as fathers' rights groups, mothers' rights groups, and parental alienation support groups, and those are also good people to ask for a referral. You want to know the name of the attorney (obviously), her fees (to know whether the attorney is within your budget), and what the person liked and did not like about the attorney (because what worked for one person may not work for another). In particular, you want to know whether the attorney understood the complex issues involved when one parent undermines and interferes in the other parent's relationship with the children and was able to effectively prevent the other parent from hijacking the legal process with unnecessary delays and false allegations. Of course, you can ask about the other aspects of working with that attorney too, such as the attorney's level of caring and communication.

(Note: If you cannot afford to pay for an attorney, you may want to start instead by finding out about free legal services in your jurisdiction. However, some private attorneys do offer what is known as pro bono services, which means that they reduce or eliminate their fees for certain clients.)

In addition to asking people for referrals to attorneys they liked, ask them which attorneys they did *not* like and what their chief complaints were. People usually like to share their horror stories, and this would be a good time to listen. Keep a list of attorneys to stay away from.

Bear in mind that sometimes it is the lead attorney at a firm who interviews new clients but a junior member of the firm who handles the majority of the work and contact with the client. Because junior members of the firm charge less per hour, you can save money that way. When asking around for the names of good attorneys, make sure to ask not only about the named partner but about the other attorneys in the firm as well.

There are many websites devoted to the problem of high-conflict custody disputes, and often on these websites you will find articles and blogs about attorneys. You may find that certain attorneys are referred to repeatedly, in either a positive or a negative light. This can help you expand your list of attorneys to consider or your list of those to avoid working with. You may also find articles and blogs written *by* attorneys, and they should give you a pretty good sense of whether the author seems to understand the gravity of the particular kind of problems in your case and has concrete and practical ideas for addressing them in court. If so, this may be a good person to add to your list of potential attorneys.

Organizations devoted to helping parents in high-conflict custody disputes, such as Parental Alienation Awareness Organization (http://www.paawareness.org), can be a useful resource. A more general resource for finding attorneys is the American Academy of Matrimonial Attorneys. On its website (http://www.aaml.org), you can search for attorneys by location and read their profiles.

Your local chapter of the Association of Family and Conciliation Courts (AFCC; http://www.afccnet.org) might host conferences devoted to the topic of high-conflict custody disputes. If you attend such a conference, which attracts parents as well as mental health and legal professionals, you may hear an attorney speak who seems to have a really good understanding of the issues. Or if you go online, you may find video clips of lectures by attorneys on various topics related to high-conflict custody disputes.

One thing to bear in mind as you create your initial list of attorneys is that you probably want an attorney who specializes in family law. An attorney who specializes in family law is more likely to be familiar with the unique legal challenges of high-conflict custody disputes than is a generalist who also practices several other types of law. In addition, you may want an expert in business law, as there is a natural overlap, especially for families with substantial wealth and assets.

If having a family lawyer is particularly important to you, you might want to consider interviewing only members of the American Academy of Matrimonial Lawyers. These attorneys must practice mostly (at least 75 percent of their cases) in the field of matrimonial law and must also work to better the field in some fashion (e.g., write authoritative papers, serve on committees), as well as have extensive trial experience. This last part may be especially important to you, because you do not want an attorney who is so unaccustomed to going to court that she pressures you into accepting a settlement in order to avoid trial. You want to trust that should your case proceed to trial, your attorney is ready, willing, and able to handle it.

Another thing to bear in mind is that some attorneys practice what is known as "collaborative law." In brief, collaborative law is when both parties agree in advance to retain lawyers trained in this particular approach to family law, who then work with the clients to achieve a binding (final) resolution that cannot later be brought back to court. Unless your ex has suggested this approach to you prior to retaining an attorney of his own (and if your ex has served you with papers, that is not the case), this is not an option for you. Selecting an attorney who prefers the collaborative approach would be a mistake, unless your ex has done the same.

A family law attorney is also more likely to know the family court judges, the family court clerks, children's attorneys, and your ex's attorney. Because all these professionals likely already know one another, if your attorney is the only one outside this network, it may be a disadvantage to your case. Certainly, if she is not one of the family law "regulars," your attorney will not be able to make an educated and informed guess as to the judge's receptivity to various strategies or approaches.

Sometimes, however, it makes sense to retain an attorney who is not part of the local "club" of family lawyers—for example, if your case is likely to involve an aggressive critique of a local psychologist's evaluation (i.e., trying to demonstrate that the custody evaluator's methods or conclusions were faulty or biased). In such circumstances, because local family lawyers and forensic psychologists frequently collaborate on multiple cases, a local family lawyer might be hesitant to aggressively cross-examine the psychologist on your case because they happen to be involved in other cases together. In this scenario, it would be wise to look outside of your geographic area for a family lawyer in order to find one who will aggressively represent your interests. Another strategy is to have a separate lawyer be "the heavy" who steps in to cross-examine the psychologist. This can be a very effective strategy, albeit an expensive one. You can retain a nationally or internationally renowned attorney to provide expert legal advice and coaching to a local attorney, especially if, for instance, there is no local family law attorney with expertise in parental alienation. Therefore, you probably want to make sure that whichever attorney you retain is comfortable working with not only a consulting attorney, but also other experts who may be needed (e.g., a parental alienation expert, an expert to rebut an unfavorable or "middle-of-the-road" custody evaluation, or an expert to review videos of child protection investigation interviews). As you seek referrals to attorneys, you can start to keep a list of potential experts to bring onto your case as well.

The Selection Process

Once you have the names of a few potential attorneys, the next step is for you to call each of them and make an appointment for an initial consultation. Some attorneys offer initial consultations for free; others do not. At the time of the appointment, it will help if you present your case in a nutshell to avoid overwhelming (or annoying) the attorney with too much detail, too much emotion, or a rambling story that does not present the essential facts in a coherent manner. An example of a brief synopsis follows:

> I am a forty-year-old mother of three girls, ages eight, nine, and eleven. I was a stay-at-home mother until about two

years ago when I went to back to work part-time as a nurse. My former husband and the father of my three children is David Johnson. He is forty-five years old and works as an investment banker for the ABC Company. I live in the marital home in Smithtown, and he lives ten minutes away in Springfield. We separated a year ago, after about six months of marital counseling. It was a reasonably mutual decision. Originally, he had the girls every other weekend and would come to the marital home every Wednesday for dinner. For the first six months or so after the separation, everything was okay, and then he started dating Cindy. In my mind, that is when things got worse and the real conflict began. Since then, he has changed lawyers (he is now represented by Jane Buckman at the Buckman-Warner firm). He has filed five motions with the court to either reduce child support or increase his parenting time. What's worse is that I think he is turning my children against me. I have a list of specific things he is doing.

I used to be represented by Charles Chapman at the Carona, Chapman, and Bates firm, but I don't think he was protecting my rights. I want to stop my ex from interfering in my relationship with my children right now, before things get any worse. My main goals are to (1) stop David from increasing his parenting time again, (2) have my parenting time enforced, even if the girls say they don't want to come, (3) compel David to answer the phone when I call so that I can talk to my girls when they are with him, (4) make him stop taking the girls to see a therapist who I think is part of the problem, and (5) not let him enroll the girls in the school in his town.

I have never had any child abuse charges filed against me. I don't drink alcohol or bring men into the home—I haven't even dated since the marriage ended—I don't do drugs, and I take good care of my daughters. The worst thing David can say about me is that the girls would rather be with him because I am sad. I don't really see the basis of that, and I don't have a history of depression, although I did cry a bit right after we broke up. Can you help me? What would your approach to my situation be, and what do you think it would cost?

If there are special issues in your situation, make sure to point them out and discuss them with the attorney. For example, if you and your partner are a gay couple, if you have been in the military, if you were born in another country, if your child is adopted, or if you have a disability that is not apparent (i.e., the attorney cannot see it for herself), it is vital that you tell your attorney from the outset so that she can factor that into her response to you. Such details may or may not be of import, but the attorney will know better than you do. The same goes for any significant liabilities, even if they are in your past, such as having a DUI, doing drugs in college, or being fired from a job. It is certain your ex knows about these things and will bring them up in court, so your potential attorney might as well know about them beforehand.

Ask the attorney whether she would like to hear about some of the ways in which your ex has undermined and interfered in your relationship with your children. You can use the seventeen primary strategies listed in the chapter 5 section "Factor 4: Your Ex Has Engaged in Parental Alienation Behaviors." Do not give long and complicated stories that require a lot of context for the attorney to understand your concern. Highlight the most egregious examples, such as lying to the children and telling them that you had an affair or were abusive when that is not the case, calling you by your first name to your children, referring to a new significant other as "Mom" or "Dad," and refusing to return the children after visitation.

Most likely, after your brief presentation, the attorney will ask you some follow-up questions in order to understand aspects of your situation that perhaps you hadn't mentioned or hadn't discussed in detail, such as your work schedule, your discipline strategy, whether you would be willing to undergo a psychological examination for depression, and whether you are currently seeing a therapist. Then, she should be able to present to you some options and explain the advantages and disadvantages of each, along with the potential costs.

At this point, you should have enough of a sense of the attorney to know whether you want to proceed with the consultation or whether you are ready to cross her off your list. You might want to end the interview if the attorney is rude or insulting to you, seems impatient or dismissive of your concerns, is frequently interrupted by phone calls, is answering e-mails or text messages while speaking with you, or makes grand promises that seem unrealistic, or if anything else makes you feel as if she doesn't really care or understand your situation. Perhaps the single most important factor is whether the attorney is able and willing to listen to you, because if the attorney is not good at listening she will be likely to miss small but significant details that could dramatically affect the outcome of your case. If you don't like her now when you are interviewing her, most likely you are not going to like her any better later, after you have paid her a retainer. However, if you do want to proceed, there are some questions you most likely will want to ask. You can enlarge the following worksheet (or download a full-scale version from http://www.newharbinger.com/30734), and fill out sections A through D as you speak with the attorney. That way, you won't forget to ask something important, nor will you forget the attorney's answers. After the meeting, take time to write down detailed notes of your impressions of the attorney in section E, because after you meet with three attorneys it may be difficult to remember what you liked and disliked about each of them.

Worksheet 3.1: Assessing a Prospective Attorney

Attorney's Name: _____

Name of Firm: _____

Date: _____

Section A: Fees and Contracts

What is the attorney's hourly rate? Is the rate by the tenth or twelfth of an hour or some other portion?

_____

How often does the attorney bill/invoice, and what is included?

_____

Can you meet the junior partner who will be assisting in the case, and how much does that person charge per hour? (It is a common and acceptable practice for a senior partner to delegate some tasks to a junior partner.)

_____

How much of a retainer is required? Is the unused portion of the retainer (if any) refunded (this is considered standard)?

_____

Is there a contract? If so, can you see a copy and have someone who is familiar with legal contracts (e.g., a friend, another attorney) review it?

_____

Section B: References

Name(s) and phone number(s) of one or two former clients, ideally ones who went through a situation similar to yours and of the same gender as you:

_____

Section C: Approach to High-Conflict Custody Cases

Has the attorney helped parents in high-conflict custody disputes before? If so, how?

_____

What does the attorney see as the major challenge in child custody disputes?

_____

How many custody cases has the attorney worked on that have gone to court (as opposed to being settled)?

_____

Does the attorney typically work with expert witnesses? If so, which ones? If not, why not?

_____

In general, are the judges in the jurisdiction in which your case will be heard receptive to the concept of parental alienation? If not, how does the attorney address that?

_____

How does the attorney stay up to date on emerging trends in high-conflict custody disputes?

_____

Is the attorney willing to aggressively advocate for your rights, even if that entails cross-examining a psychologist whom the attorney has worked with before or filing a motion to recuse a judge (rare, but sometimes necessary)?

_____

Has the attorney ever handled a case in which your ex's lawyer was the opposing counsel? If so, how did that work out?

_____

How many cases, or what percentage of cases, has the attorney worked on that involved child protection and/or domestic violence services and relevant laws?

_____

Based on what you have told the attorney, how does he or she think he or she would be able to help you, and what does he or she think the major obstacles would be?

_____

Section D: Questions You Have About Other Aspects of Your Case (e.g., finances, moving away)

_____

_____

_____

Section E: Your Impressions

Did the attorney appear to care about your thoughts and feelings?

   (not at all) 0   1   2   3   4 (very much)

Comments: _____

Did the attorney give you his or her undivided attention?

   (not at all) 0   1   2   3   4 (very much)

Comments: _____

Did the attorney appear compassionate?

   (not at all) 0   1   2   3   4 (very much)

Comments: _____

Did the attorney seem familiar with the issues relevant to your case (e.g., moving away, parental alienation, grandparents' rights)?

   (not at all) 0   1   2   3   4 (very much)

Comments: _____

Ratings and comments for any other areas you feel are important (competence, diligence, communication, advocacy, advising, etc.):

_____

_____

_____

Hopefully, you will like and feel comfortable with at least one of the three attorneys you interview, and you will proceed to a retainer. If you do not, select another three to interview.

Self-Care Tip

Selecting an attorney will have a major effect on your case—and on your life, at least in the short run. Make sure to give yourself plenty of time to get a feel for the various attorneys whom you are interviewing. Trust yourself to know when you have found the right attorney so that you don't make a hasty decision. Talk over the pros and cons of each attorney with someone you trust.

Consider Hiring a Mental Health Consultant

Instead of undertaking the attorney selection and retention process yourself, you could hire a mental health consultant to help you with this (and many other tasks). In *Working with Alienated Children and Families: A Clinical Guidebook*, J. Michael Bone and S. Richard Sauber (2012), two experts in high-conflict custody disputes, describe the mental health consultant's role in detail specifically for parental alienation cases, and their points are applicable to any high-conflict custody dispute. In brief, a mental health consultant is a qualified and trained mental health professional who has extensive experience with the psychological issues involved in high-conflict custody disputes, as well as experience helping with strategy and interacting with lawyers. The role of the mental health consultant is to help you navigate the legal and mental health systems as your case proceeds. We will explore the process of finding, selecting, and working with a mental health consultant in detail in the next chapter.

Working with Your Attorney

Whether you retain an attorney on your own or with the assistance of a mental health consultant, this step is only the beginning of your work together. In this next section, we present some ideas and pointers for working with your attorney to maximize her effectiveness and your satisfaction with the outcomes.

Communication

Because attorneys typically bill in increments of an hour, for attorneys who bill in five-minute increments, any task that takes between one and five minutes will cost you one-twelfth of the hourly rate. Don't be surprised if your attorney's invoices list charges for things such as forwarding mail to you and answering brief questions on the phone. With a high enough hourly rate, even these minor tasks can cost a lot of money. Attorneys work in billable hours, and so every minute of the day needs to be accounted for and charged to one client or another. Obviously, you want to be mindful of that as you proceed. You probably want to keep a log of all of your contact with your attorney so that you can compare your log to your attorney's invoices and ensure that you are not getting billed for time not spent on your case. (Obviously, you cannot know about time your attorney spends on your case when you are not present, but you can keep track of time spent on phone calls and in meetings with you.)

Some parents in custody disputes complain that they have difficulty reaching their attorney, especially during an emergency. Make sure that you know how to reach your attorney during an emergency, as well as what kind of routine communication (voice messages, e-mails, etc.) she prefers. Keep a log of the times you tried to reach your attorney and could not do so, to make sure that there isn't an emerging pattern of neglect. For example, how many times do you have to call and leave a message before you hear back? If the answer is more than you are comfortable with, it is better to discuss this early in the process rather than letting it go until there is a true legal emergency and your attorney is not as responsive as you need her to be. It would probably be wise to discuss your concerns and experiences with others to see whether your expectations are realistic. For example, if you need to speak to your attorney on a Friday but she is typically in court on Fridays, it is possible that you will not get through and may not hear back until the weekend or Monday morning, since cell phones must be turned off in court. Perhaps you can leave a message with your attorney's office in this case, and the office will send a text message to the assistant (if the assistant is in court with your attorney), and perhaps the assistant will inform the attorney of your desire to touch base. But it may be that the assistant deems your need not as urgent as the need for the attorney to focus on the case at hand in order to meet the needs of *that* client.

To avoid unnecessary frustration and disappointment, find out from your attorney which situations you should inform her about on an ASAP basis (because timely action may be required) and which situations it is okay to wait until the next business day to inform her about. You can present common scenarios such as these and ask how you should communicate with her about them:

- Your ex refuses to return the children to you.

- Your children tell you that your ex is taking them to see a therapist.

- You find out that your ex has become engaged.

- You find out that your child was taken to the hospital and you weren't notified.

Whereas any of these scenarios would naturally be very alarming to you, not all of them would warrant an emergency phone call to your attorney. You might feel extremely upset and anxious in such scenarios, but that doesn't mean that your attorney would be the right person to contact for immediate assistance.

That being said, it is important that you inform your attorney of any significant events in a timely fashion (just not necessarily on an emergency basis). Significant events include any limits imposed on your parenting time or access to your children, any allegations of child abuse or domestic violence, any police involvement (e.g., you called the police to escort you, your ex called the police to complain about you), physical altercations with your children, mental health or physical health problems of your children that occurred on your watch, and any changes in your household or your ex's household (e.g., her parents moved in, a boyfriend moved out).

As you live your life as a parent in a high-conflict custody dispute, questions about your legal situation may pop into your head. Keep a running list of these questions on hand at all times so that when your attorney calls, you can reference them. With this list, if your attorney calls at an inopportune time for you, catching you off guard, you won't have to rely on your memory to get all of your questions answered. Make sure to write down the answers. When you are anxious (as you probably are when it comes to your legal matters), it is more difficult to think logically and retain what is being said. You may find that shortly after you hang up the phone, you have absolutely no memory of what your attorney said. Writing down the answers will prevent you from losing important information.

Preparing and Delivering the Evidence to Your Attorney

Part of working with an attorney is preparing and delivering evidence relevant to your case. Although we will review this topic in depth in chapter 5, there are a few guidelines you should begin following immediately.

As we will reiterate throughout the book, make sure to always keep a duplicate set of whatever documents you submit to your attorney. Also, make sure that the documents that you keep in your home are not accessible to your children, as this could reflect badly on you in court. If you store them on your computer, make sure that both the computer and the files are protected by passwords that are new since the separation and difficult to guess. Back the files up off-site to protect them from being lost or destroyed, which could be catastrophic for your case. Protect your portable devices (laptops, scan drives, and so forth) from being moved to another location.

Deciding Whether to Retain Expert Witnesses

Your attorney can help you decide whether you need one or more expert witnesses on your case, such as a parental alienation expert, an expert to rebut an unfavorable or "middle-of-the-road" custody evaluation, an expert to advise on an appropriate therapeutic intervention, or an expert to review videos of child protection investigation interviews. Your attorney may be able to recommend specific experts he has worked with before and in some instances can function as the liaison with the expert (retaining the expert, making payments to the expert and then billing you, discussing the parameters of the charge, etc.). In other instances, you may be the one to find, interview, select, retain, pay, and in all respects interact with the expert witness (although this can introduce potential bias or the appearance of bias into your relationship, which can become problematic later in court). When your attorney retains the expert witness, legal privilege is maintained, which can be important for your legal strategy. (Legal privilege means that what is said between the attorney and the expert does not have to be shared in court as part of the discovery process unless the expert issues an expert report for trial purposes.) Ask your attorney what her typical approach to bringing expert witnesses on board is. Some elements of her approach may be dictated by custom and habit;

others may be based on the jurisdiction in which your case is being heard. There is developing jurisprudence on the need to fully document all matters that went into the expert's analysis, and to make that file available to all parties in the case prior to the expert testifying. We strongly advise that your attorney, and not you as the client, retains the expert witness. However, we will discuss hiring and retaining an expert witness yourself in chapter 7.

Regardless of who retains the expert witness, your attorney must allocate several hours to making preparations with that expert prior to court. There are two main reasons to spend time in preparation:

- So that the attorney can review principles of effective testimony with the expert witness

- So that the expert witness can review the theoretical principles about which she will be testifying with the attorney

It is possible that an attorney could suggest forgoing this step, but that could result in a poor outcome. Testifying in court represents the intersection of legal strategy and expert knowledge, and so each person has something essential to teach the other. One of the things that could happen if such a preparation session does not occur is the expert responding differently than anticipated to a hypothetical question from your attorney while on the stand. For example, your attorney could ask, "Isn't it true, Dr. Jones, that if I told you that the children asked their mother whether they could stay an extra day with their father, this would be an example of parental alienation?" With no other information to go on, the expert witness would have to respond "Possibly," which would not be helpful to your attorney or your case. It is ideal if the expert and your attorney can review the key concepts related to the case so that the attorney can ask questions that will elicit the necessary information from the expert on the witness stand.

Likewise, the expert may need to be reminded and prepped about key aspects of testifying—aside from the content. For example, in some jurisdictions an expert witness is permitted to have his notes with him on the witness stand (as long as opposing counsel can have a copy as well). In others he can refer to his report only if he asks the court using specific language—for example, in Massachusetts, the expert witness would have to say, "I need to have my memory refreshed," and then peruse his report. In addition, it would be helpful for your attorney to share pointers regarding her particular style of conducting a direct examination. Some attorneys feel strongly about stylistic aspects of the direct examination and cross-examination or know what the judge is bothered by in experts and can provide the expert with advice and style tips to help him maximize the effectiveness of his testimony in that particular courtroom.

When the expert and your attorney have a preparation session, you will be paying both of them for their time. Obviously, this can be an expensive proposition, but this is not a time to cut corners to save money, because it is hard to imagine a more important meeting than this one. Your attorney might also recommend that you hire a mental health consultant to provide behind-the-scenes advice to both you and your attorney on selecting, working with, and prepping expert witnesses.

Helping Prepare Your Case

No one cares more about your case than you do. It is not likely that your attorney is up at night mulling over the ins and outs of your case, no matter how compassionate and dedicated he is. Because of your vested interest in achieving a good outcome, you have the most energy to devote to your case and the most reason to be diligent. You also know the facts and details better than anyone else. Therefore, it behooves you to offer to assist your attorney with the preparation of your case in any way that would be useful. This is the key: it must be useful to your attorney. Otherwise, you may spend time preparing documents that are of no use to him. Useful pursuits may include gathering scholarly articles on topics related to your case (e.g., when one parent moves away, parental alienation, emotional abuse) and organizing your documents (assuming that you have not done so already). Anything you do to save work and effort on the part of your attorney will save you money, so you will benefit in that way as well. In addition, you will have the satisfaction of helping yourself.

Conclusion

Selecting the right attorney for your case is a very important step. Give yourself time to make a careful and thoughtful decision. Remember, it is essential that your attorney understands the key issues involved in your case and be familiar with the common approaches to those issues.

In working with your attorney, there are several things you can do to make the attorney's job easier, help your case, and avoid disappointment and frustration. Needless to say, your attorney is not completely responsible for the outcome of your case. Your attorney might put on a fantastic case for you, but the judge—for his own reasons, like biases, comfort level, pressures, and so on—might not be receptive to it.

A mental health consultant might be a helpful addition to your team as a liaison between you and your attorney. This is the subject of the next chapter.

CHAPTER 4

Finding and Working with the Right Mental Health Consultant

Many parents in high-conflict custody disputes work with a mental health consultant to help them navigate the legal and mental health systems they will encounter. A mental health consultant is a mental health professional with an advanced degree in psychology or social work from an accredited institution and with several years of experience in the field of high-conflict custody disputes who works "behind the scenes" to help clients anticipate and meet the various demands of their case. "Behind the scenes" means that the person you hire as your mental health consultant will not be testifying, so you don't have to notify opposing counsel of this person's involvement. Although this person is helping you navigate the *legal* system, we use the term "mental health consultant" to emphasize the psychological aspects of the work: helping you understand the psychology of the custody evaluation, helping you understand the way you are perceived in the community, helping your attorney understand the psychological aspects of your testimony, and so forth. The mental health consultant is your personal guide through the maze of the high-conflict custody dispute and can help you determine how to present yourself.

We know from research that many parents in high-conflict custody disputes feel that their attorney alone cannot provide them with the guidance and support they need (Baker 2010). They don't know whether they have the right attorney for their case, and they have questions that the typical attorney cannot answer. "Mental health consultant" is a new role in custody disputes, one that has evolved to address those needs and concerns of litigants that are outside the domain of therapists and attorneys. The purpose of this chapter is to help you identify whether a mental health consultant is right for you.

According to Bone and Sauber (2012, 76–78), a mental health consultant can help in high-conflict custody disputes by intervening to prevent various "points of slippage" in the family court system. A point of slippage is defined as any way in which the case may not go in your favor (i.e., slip away from you) for reasons other than its merits.

Points of Slippage

As you may already know, the family court system is highly unpredictable in its rulings. Two judges may come to very different conclusions based on the same set of facts and evidence. For example, one judge may conclude that a parent deserves to have been rejected by his children; another may conclude that the rejected parent has done nothing to warrant his children's rejection and that the principal cause is the other parent's undermining efforts. Likewise, two judges may come to the same conclusion—for example, that one parent has turned the children against the other parent—but make very different rulings based on their beliefs about how to handle these types of situations (one judge might impose sanctions against the interfering parent and order an intensive reunification program for the children and rejected parent; another might choose to "let nature take its course"). Family court judges have tremendous discretion. That means that they can rely on their own thoughts and feelings about a case to make their rulings. A judge's beliefs that would lead her to be disinclined to see your perspective can be considered a point of slippage.

A second point of slippage in the family court system is that family court is (appropriately) oriented toward the protection of women and children. Therefore, allegations of danger or threat of danger to children automatically receive the court's full attention on an emergency basis and are usually given the benefit of the doubt. Thus, one parent, by creating the impression of danger, can immediately change the course of a high-conflict custody dispute. Judges are likely to err on the side of caution if there is any concern that the children will be unsafe with a parent or that a parent will be subjected to domestic violence. Unfortunately, your ex's misuse of this bias toward safety can result in the case slipping away from you through no fault of your own.

Third, decisions about children's safety and their best interest involve psychological principles, but the decisions themselves are made by non-psychologists. State child protection agencies tend to be underfunded and understaffed, leading to a reliance on workers who have limited psychological training and insight. The person investigating a claim of child abuse or neglect may not be trained to distinguish between true and false accusations made by children and may be unaware that children who are the subject of a high-conflict custody dispute can be coached to make false allegations against a parent. Likewise, despite the fact that psychological issues are of primary importance in child custody cases, the judge usually is not a trained psychologist and may be unprepared to properly evaluate the truthfulness of the claims the parents make about each other.

Yet another point of slippage is that both sides may bring expert witnesses to convince the judge of one or more critical aspects of their case. Some of these experts may be "hired guns" who—for the right price—will testify to almost any point of view. Being a "hired gun" is obviously unethical, but it is not illegal. A point of slippage in your case could occur if the other side has retained an impressive expert witness who will support your ex's false version of events.

You can bring a mental health consultant—a trained mental health professional with expertise in family law—onto your team to help you understand and address these points of slippage before they adversely affect your case.

The Mental Health Consultant's Role

Your mental health consultant can be involved in many key tasks during your custody dispute and essentially work with you step by step to craft the most compelling case possible.

Helping You Hire Your Attorney

Your mental health consultant can help you find the right attorney for your case. Most likely, he already knows some good attorneys and can suggest one to you. If not, he can help you identify the qualities you are seeking in an attorney, can generate a list of possible attorneys, and can even interview them for you. Your mental health consultant can also look up an attorney's record of wins and losses and determine whether that attorney is a skilled litigator.

Working with Your Attorney to Develop a Legal Strategy

Once the attorney has been hired, your mental health consultant can interact with the attorney on your behalf, professional to professional. She can work with your attorney to develop a legal strategy that makes sense for your case. She may know more about legal options in a particular area (such as one parent moving away or parental alienation) than your attorney and can provide suggestions based on past experiences; she may be more up to date on intervention options than your attorney and able to recommend what to ask the court for; and she should be able to reduce the pressure you place on your attorney by absorbing and addressing some of your concerns.

Helping You Work with Your Attorney

Your mental health consultant can also help you work effectively with your attorney by helping you clarify your questions and concerns. He can also assist you in selecting and organizing your evidence by combing through your documents and determining which ones will be most useful to your attorney. Based on his experience with a range of attorneys, he can also help you develop appropriate expectations of your attorney. He can let you know whether you are being too lax or asking too much of your attorney and help keep your expectations reasonable.

Helping You Select an Expert Witness or Other Expert

Should an expert witness or other type of expert be necessary for your case, your mental health consultant can help you identify appropriate options. Most likely, she knows who the experts are in any given field and has worked with them enough to know who does well on the stand, who writes credible reports, and whom a particular judge will be amenable to. She can also conduct initial interviews of various potential experts, to avoid the appearance of bias that is created when a client interviews her own experts. In this way, she can help you bring together the best team possible.

Helping Prepare the Expert

Once an expert witness has been retained on your case, your mental health consultant can help prepare that person for her tasks.

He can organize documents for her and can help develop the proper expert witness strategy. For example, if an expert witness has been retained to rebut a custody evaluation report, your mental health consultant can read the report and discuss it with the expert witness. He can provide suggestions about how the expert witness might want to approach the task and could conduct legal or psychological research to assist the expert witness.

Helping You Select and Prepare Your Collateral Contacts

Most likely, you will need to identify and prepare "collateral contacts" for your case. These are people who will be asked to testify on your behalf at a hearing or trial and/or be available to discuss your family situation with a custody evaluator.

The people whom you would naturally think of as the best collateral contacts may actually not be the best ones for your case. Your passionate supporters may appear to be too emotional or biased; others may appear too stilted or emotionally distant. There are many factors that go into finding and preparing the right collateral contacts, and a mental health consultant can help you comb through your list to identify the handful of people who will be most effective for your case.

Helping You Prepare for the Custody Evaluation

Your mental health consultant can help you anticipate the various components of the custody evaluation and help you feel ready for them. He can explain the process from the evaluator's point of view, helping you understand what the goals are so that you can provide the evaluator with the information she needs to conduct her work. He can help you anticipate and avoid common pitfalls, such as being overly anxious or trying too hard.

Helping Your Attorney Understand the Methods and Results of the Custody Evaluation

If the custody evaluator's recommendations are not supportive of your position, and especially if you believe that this is because they are biased or flawed, your mental health consultant can review the evaluator's methodology and conclusions in order to develop an effective rebuttal to the report. For example, perhaps the best approach is to depose the evaluator to expose her weaknesses and errors. Perhaps it makes sense to hire an expert to provide a written and/or oral critique of the evaluator's report and work. Your mental health consultant will know the various options and can steer you in the right direction. She can also explain some of the technical parts of the report (e.g., test results, comparisons to norms, diagnostic terminology) to you and your attorney.

Helping You and Your Attorney Prepare for a Restraining Order Hearing

If your ex has filed papers seeking a temporary restraining order (TRO) against you or has filed a motion to turn a TRO into a permanent restraining order (RO), your mental health consultant can explain to you and your attorney the long-term consequences of consenting to the order versus contesting it in court. Should you decide to fight the order, your mental health consultant can help you prepare the proper evidence and collateral contacts for that hearing. A restraining order is pivotal in any high-conflict custody dispute, and often the issue does not receive proper attention. Your attorney may suggest that you sign the order to avoid having to go to court, but this is usually a mistake to be avoided at all costs. A finding of domestic violence, which is what the granting of a restraining order amounts to, is a black mark against you for the rest of the case. It creates the impression that the judge weighed and considered the facts and decided that you were a perpetrator of domestic violence. This can contribute to a negative image of you in the eyes of your children, as well as in the community, because the general public is not aware (a) of how easy it is for a person to be granted a TRO or (b) that if the accused fails to show up for the hearing, a TRO is most likely going to be turned into a permanent restraining order.

Helping You and Your Attorney Understand the Judge

Your mental health consultant can also investigate the specific record of the judge assigned to your case. The more that you know about the judge's history and potential biases, the more effectively you and your attorney can make decisions. This is akin to an attorney hiring a jury consultant to "get inside the head" of the jury. In family court, where there are no juries, you essentially have a jury of one: the judge. It therefore makes a great deal of sense to find out as much as possible about the specific judge assigned to your case.

Some lawyers are inclined to undervalue such knowledge due to their legal training. Lawyers are, after all, trained on the principle of "blind justice under the law," meaning that decisions should be based on the law, not the person making the decision. However, in the case of family law, given the considerable discretion at the judge's disposal, the judge's biases and history are very important to know. In family law, all the things that are not supposed to matter—bias, personal experience, and so on—do matter, a lot.

The Disadvantages of a Mental Health Consultant

With all these benefits, you might think that it is always a good idea to bring a mental health consultant into your high-conflict custody case, but there are potential downsides as well. First, a highly qualified mental health consultant will certainly not be cheap. Some mental health consultants offer task-related fees, and others charge by the hour, but most likely you will want yours to perform multiple tasks, and this could significantly add to your overall up-front costs. Even if your mental health consultant is a licensed clinician, there is very little chance your health insurance company will reimburse you for his fees, since he is not providing you with mental health treatment per se. Moreover, even if the judge awards you "attorney's fees" (which seems to be rare), the work of non-attorney experts is usually not covered. Thus, the cost of a mental health consultant is significant and most likely to be out of pocket. Bone and Sauber (2012) point out that the up-front cost of a mental health consultant may be offset by a reduction in costs incurred later due to incompetent or underprepared attorneys and misguided legal strategies; that is, you may pay more initially but end up saving money that you would have had to spend if you had not had the consultant's help. However, it is difficult to estimate how much this will be.

Second, there is always the potential for your attorney and your mental health consultant to disagree about overall legal strategy (e.g., should you ask for a transfer of custody or not?) or about a particular detail of your case (e.g., should you file a motion for lack of compliance now, or should you wait?). Ideally, they will know how to get along and how best to resolve their differences, but if not, you might be caught in the middle, worried that to side with one will hurt or anger the other.

The third disadvantage is not strictly a disadvantage of having a mental health consultant, but the fact that there are unscrupulous individuals who may claim to be experts in one or more aspects of a high-conflict custody dispute (e.g., false allegations of sexual abuse, parental alienation, preparing for a custody evaluation) when in fact they are not trained professionals. We recommend extreme care and caution when deciding whom to hire as your consultant. Make sure that the person you select has credentials and training pertinent to the areas in question and a solid reputation in the field. (Since mental health consulting is an emerging field, at this time we are unfortunately unable to recommend resources or organizations for you to check with.)

Finding the Right Mental Health Consultant

We recommend that you hire someone who has extensive experience working in high-conflict custody cases in a related capacity—for example, as a guardian ad litem (which may mean different things in different jurisdictions) or a custody evaluator. Look for this person to have an affiliation with a professional body and ethical guidelines to which he must adhere. We strongly urge you to be wary of anyone who claims to function as a mental health consultant but who has no credentials other than being a parent involved in a high-conflict custody dispute himself. Such people's experience is simply too limited and too influenced by their own personal journey for them to be very helpful for you.

Referral Sources

Whether you are in immediate need of advice or not, it is time to make a list of potential mental health consultants. All the suggestions for finding an appropriate attorney apply here as well: Check with organizations devoted to a cause related to your areas of concern (fathers' rights, mothers' rights, false allegations of abuse, etc.). If you know someone who is dealing with a similar situation who has worked with a mental health consultant and been satisfied with that person's compassion, diligence, and helpfulness, you will want to start by getting that professional's name. Again, you can contact parent support groups in your community and go online to find referrals, making note of the mental health consultants whom people had a good experience with and those with whom people seem dissatisfied. Websites devoted to topics related to high-conflict custody disputes are also an excellent source of names of potential mental health consultants (although that particular term will not be used in most cases—you might look for someone referred to as "parental alienation consultant" or "custody consultant"). If you cannot find a mental health consultant near you, keep in mind that it is not essential that you work with a consultant in person, although that could certainly be helpful.

The Selection Process

Once you have the names of a few possible mental health consultants, the next step is to call and make an appointment for an initial consultation with each one. The initial consultation, which may or may not be free, will most likely be on the phone. You should consider what is appropriate to cover in this initial exploratory call. For example, the purpose of the call is most likely to determine whether the person is a good fit for you and your case, not to pick his brain extensively about legal strategy. At the time of the appointment, it will help if you present your case in a nutshell so as to avoid overwhelming the person with too much detail, too much emotion, or a story that is out of order and does not present the essential facts in a coherent manner. An example of a brief synopsis follows:

> My name is David Cline, and I am a forty-five-year-old father of thirteen-year-old twin boys. My former wife is Maria Cline. She is represented by the Wilson and Cane law firm in Bristol, New Hampshire. We have had ongoing litigation for the past five years since the separation. I recently parted ways with my attorney, Lucy Warren. I am seeking a professional to help me find the right attorney and work with that attorney to plan my case. Jack Faller suggested I contact you, since he found you helpful on his case. Can you review with me your procedures, services, and fees?

Most likely, after your brief presentation, the person will ask you some follow-up questions in order to understand aspects of your case that perhaps you hadn't mentioned or didn't cover in sufficient detail, such as why you parted ways with your prior attorney, where you are in the legal process (e.g., is there a pending motion?), and whether you have worked with other consultants and experts. Then he should be able to talk about what his role in your case might look like and the potential cost.

At this point, you should have enough of a sense of the person to know whether you want to proceed with the consultation or whether you are ready to cross him off your list (the same reasons for eliminating an attorney apply). If you do want to proceed, the following worksheet (you can download it in full-scale form at http://www.newharbinger.com/30734) can help. First there are questions to help guide you during the interview, then questions to help you rate your impressions and jot down any notes afterward.

Worksheet 4.1: Assessing a Prospective Mental Health Consultant

Consultant's Name: _____

Date: _____

What are this person's educational credentials?

_____

Has this person provided training and workshops to other mental health and legal professionals on topics related to your case?

_____

Has this person published articles in academic and clinical journals on issues related to high-conflict custody disputes?

_____

What does this person charge by the hour? (There is no set fee, but it would be reasonable to expect at least $250 an hour if the person is a nationally recognized expert in the field.)

_____

Does this person have references you can speak to? (Write names and contact info.)

_____

Did this person appear to care about your thoughts and feelings?

(not at all) 0   1   2   3   4 (very much)

Comments: _____

Did this person give you his or her undivided attention?

(not at all) 0   1   2   3   4 (very much)

Comments: _____

Did this person seem compassionate?

(not at all) 0   1   2   3   4 (very much)

Comments: _____

Did this person seem familiar with the issues relevant to your case (e.g., moving away, parental alienation, grandparents' rights)?

(not at all) 0   1   2   3   4 (very much)

Comments: _____

Any other ratings or comments you feel are important:

_____

_____

Hopefully, you will like and feel comfortable with at least one of the people you interview, and you will proceed to a retainer. You should know that there is no clear ethical guideline about a mental health consultant speaking to both parties on a case, so you probably want to ask whether anyone from the "other side" has already contacted this person.

Self-Care Tip

A mental health consultant might seem like an extravagant expense, and you may consider not hiring one in order to save money. If so, we urge you to make sure that this is a reasoned decision and not one made out of fear or a sense that you don't deserve all the help and guidance you can get. Talk the decision over with someone who can help you weigh the advantages and disadvantages. A very real consideration is that, as mentioned, a mental health consultant might help you avoid errors that can be even more costly. Although hiring a mental health consultant is an initial expense, this person's wisdom may prevent the need for "rehabilitative litigation" (filing motions to undo mistakes that were made earlier due to strategic error and naïveté). Give yourself permission to bring on someone who can really help and guide you.

Getting Started Working with Your Mental Health Consultant

In this section, we present some ideas and pointers for working with your mental health consultant to maximize her effectiveness and your satisfaction with the outcomes.

Communication

As you get started, it will be helpful to know your mental health consultant's preferred mode of communication with clients (i.e., phone or e-mail), during what hours it is acceptable to call her (pay particular attention to any time zone difference), and her typical response time to e-mails and voice mails. Make sure that you know what would constitute an emergency and what would not so that you can provide her with timely information to help protect your interests.

Because a mental health consultant is both a handholder and an informed adviser, be prepared for the fact that your mental health consultant can and should bill you for time spent comforting you and helping you with your emotional responses.

Preparing and Delivering the Evidence

Your mental health consultant may want to review all of your documents before you submit them to your attorney, or he may want a duplicate set of anything you send or have sent to your attorney. Ask what works for him. Either way, see chapter 5 for an in-depth discussion of how to prepare your evidence, and make sure to keep a duplicate set of all documents you submit.

Conclusion

Deciding whether to retain a mental health consultant to help you in your high-conflict custody dispute is an important decision and not one you should make lightly. There are many advantages, but also some disadvantages, especially if you hire someone who claims to have more experience and expertise than he really has. Give yourself permission to make a careful and thoughtful decision.

Like your attorney, your mental health consultant is not completely responsible for the outcomes of your case. Your mental health consultant might help you and your attorney put on a compelling case for you, but the judge—for her own reasons (biases, comfort level, pressures, and so on)—might not be receptive to it.

CHAPTER 5

Documenting Your Case
for Your Attorney

Once you have an attorney who seems able to competently and diligently represent your interests, you need to prepare and deliver your evidence to her in a manner that will help her effectively meet your needs. Your attorney needs to review the evidence before she can do any of the following:

- Give you feedback about your situation and your legal options

- Help you decide whether you should proceed with a legal matter

- Use those documents in preparing your case

By evidence, we mean documents, video and audio recordings, statements by other people, and any other items (photographs, birthday cards your children made for you, etc.) that demonstrate the nature of your relationship with your ex and the children and help support your theory of the case.

Principles of Preparing Your Evidence

The more organized and coherent your materials are, the more easily and effectively your attorney will be able to assist you. Just as you don't want to dump a bunch of receipts into your accountant's lap, you don't want to deliver a jumbled mass of pages to your attorney. Since you are paying your attorney by the hour, you will save money (and your attorney some aggravation) if you organize your evidence in a coherent manner.

Try not to overwhelm your attorney with written commentary on the documents, and try to keep your comments as objective as possible. Also, be honest about your weaknesses and your former spouse's strengths. It is pointless and actually counterproductive to withhold vital information from your attorney, especially about weaknesses in your parenting or in your proposed parenting plan. These weaknesses will surely be revealed eventually, and it will be better for you if your attorney is prepared. If you are a neat freak, if you are a slob, if you drink too much, if you looked at pornography online, if you had an affair, or if you loaned money to a friend and never got it back, you need to share that information with your attorney—no matter how embarrassed you feel about it—if it has any bearing on your moral character and/or your ability to parent your children. In this situation, knowledge is truly power. This holds true even for things that you think are not relevant, such as smoking pot in high school or failing a course in college. Let your attorney decide what is and is not relevant, and err on the side of sharing too much. Your attorney will know how to best position any weaknesses in your history.

Regardless of what organizational structure you use (we present several options below), you should also prepare for your attorney a fact sheet and chronology of events, to serve as a handy reference. Focus on major milestones in your family and any significant events in which you, your ex, or both of you failed to meet the children's needs. You can use the following outline:

- Vital statistics about you
  - Name
  - Date of birth
  - City of birth
  - Parents' names

- Name and number of siblings
- Date graduated high school
- College attended
- Date graduated or left college and degree received
- Graduate training received (schools, degrees, and dates)

- Vital statistics about your ex (same as above)

- Chronology of your relationship
  - Date you met
  - How long you dated
  - Date of wedding
  - Location of wedding

- Important events since you married
  - Addresses of homes you have lived in, with dates you lived there
  - Jobs each of you has held (include title, employer, approximate salary, full-time or part-time)
  - Dates of birth of each child, along with name, gender, and current age
  - Any prior motions, court dates, and court orders
  - Dates of any marital separations
  - Any involvement of police or child protection services

- Any defining moments in your custody dispute to date (any major incidents that are likely to be presented as the reason your children don't want to see you)

- Major events in the children's lives and in the parents' lives (with explanation of how they may have affected the children)

This information will help orient your attorney as she reviews your evidence, and it is the kind of information that your attorney will want to present to the judge via direct examination of you and your collateral witnesses in a hearing or trial. The real goal is to have the judge get to know you—to be familiar and comfortable with you, which can favorably affect your case. Too often in family court, attorneys do not give their clients the potential advantage of the judge's having this sort of personal knowledge of them.

Options for Organizing Your Evidence

In this section, we present three ways to organize your documents for your attorney (and experts, should you hire any):

- By type and subject and chronology

- By the best interest of the child (BIC) standards of the jurisdiction in which your case is being heard

- By a five-factor model of parental alienation (should that be relevant for your case)

It is wise to ask your attorney (and any experts on your case) which organizational structure would work best. If your attorney doesn't have a strong opinion, you could describe the various options and see which one she thinks will be helpful. Your attorney might want all three types, but that would obviously involve duplicating many documents and could potentially be cumbersome.

By Type and Chronology

When preparing your evidence by type and chronology, you should create a binder (or several binders, depending on how much evidence you have) divided into the following categories.

COURT DOCUMENTS

Include copies of all pleadings and prior motions, cross motions, orders, stipulated agreements, affidavits, and transcripts from prior hearings and trials and depositions. These should be in chronological order, from earliest to most recent.

COMMUNICATION WITH YOUR EX, YOUR EX'S NEW PARTNER, OR RELEVANT THIRD PARTIES

Include copies of e-mails that can be authenticated by an expert if necessary (as opposed to text that has been cut and pasted); screen shots of text messages (some telephone companies can provide the content of text messages sent to and from phones in their network); and audio recordings of voice messages, phone calls, or meetings (as long as your attorney has informed you that such recordings are admissible in the jurisdiction in which your case will be heard). Arrange them from earliest to most recent and also by topic—that is, you want two sets, one of which is strictly chronological and one of which is organized by relevant topic. It may be helpful to provide a spreadsheet of the various communications by date and by topic (e.g., scheduling difficulties, hostile and denigrating attitudes). Transcripts of any audio recordings may also be helpful.

REPORTS FROM MENTAL HEALTH PROFESSIONALS

Place all letters or formal evaluations, even ones that are unflattering to you or those that you believe to be biased and incorrect, concerning you, your ex, or the children in chronological order from earliest to most recent.

DOCUMENTS PERTAINING TO CHILD PROTECTION SERVICES

Include all contact with child protection services, even for findings that were unfounded/not indicated. If you have access to any recordings of interviews of your children, this could be particularly helpful for ascertaining whether proper interview techniques were used.

SUPERVISED VISITATION OR SUPERVISED TRANSITION CENTER REPORTS

Include all progress notes or communication about your supervised visits or attempts to exercise parenting time with your children.

DOCUMENTS PERTAINING TO DOMESTIC VIOLENCE

Include all communication regarding reports and/or findings with respect to domestic violence, especially any motions with respect to temporary or permanent restraining orders.

COMMUNICATION TO AND FROM YOUR CHILDREN

Include letters, texts, or e-mails from your children to or about you and your extended family that are particularly positive or negative (e.g., Mother's Day cards extolling your virtues, letters to the judge alleging that you were abusive).

FALSE ALLEGATIONS AND INTENTIONAL MISREPRESENTATIONS ABOUT YOU

Catalog all false allegations, whether explicit (lies about you to child protection services or the police) or innuendo (lies about you to the children, neighbors, coaches, teachers, etc.), in a chart or spreadsheet, along with concrete evidence of their lack of veracity, to expose the misinformation that is being propagated about you. This "lie list" can be a powerful document and one that is very useful to a good attorney. Not only does it absolve you of whatever your ex is accusing you of, but also it demonstrates your ex's intentions to disrupt your relationship with your children. These false allegations are the same lies your children are being told about you, whether directly or indirectly. If you can establish that these are, in fact, lies and that this is the source of your conflict with your children, you will have established a strong case that your ex's behavior has had a negative effect on your relationship with your children.

For example, if your ex has fabricated a concern about your "reckless" driving, include a copy of your driver safety record. If your ex has falsely accused you of misappropriating your children's college funds, include relevant bank statements. If your ex has alleged that you have a track record of failing at work, bring in your personnel file showing your history of positive evaluations and promotions. If your ex has minimized your contribution to your children's education and development, bring in photographs that show your involvement.

Make sure that you have a duplicate copy of the binder(s) that you deliver to your attorney so that the two of you can refer to the same document at the same time (e.g., "binder 1, tab 3, page 20"). You could also scan the entire record of evidence and save it as a single file, for ease of transfer and access.

DOCUMENTS PERTAINING TO THE EDUCATION OR SCHOOLING OF THE CHILDREN

This binder would include all documents pertaining to the educational well-being and functioning of the children, including report cards, evaluations, awards, attendance sheets, and disability or educational/learning diagnoses.

RECORDING BINDER

All audio and video recordings relevant to your case will be included in this binder. Examples include copies of answering machine messages, home movies, and sexual abuse investigation tapes.

SPECIAL TOPICS BINDER

This binder would include documents pertaining to any special topics relevant in the case—for example, medical conditions of the parents or children, diagnoses that are in dispute (e.g., one parent believes a child is autistic but the other does not), one of the parents is a medical doctor and is treating the children, or one of the parents has had an affair.

By Best Interests of the Child Standards

Each jurisdiction has its own list of factors for judges to consider when deciding on the best interests of the children. The factors that could be considered in the jurisdiction in which your case will be heard include the following:

- Each parent's wishes
- The children's wishes (with or without mention of specific age cutoff)
- Who the primary caretaker was prior to the divorce
- The quality of the children's interactions with each parent
- The children's interactions with each other and other family members
- The children's adjustment to the home, school, and community
- Each parent's compliance with the rights and responsibilities of parenting
- Any military care plan
- Any intention of either parent to relocate
- Any involvement of the children by either parent in parental disputes
- The geographic distance between the parents' homes

- The length of time the children have been in the home environment

- The permanence of the family unit

- Each parent's mental and physical health

- Each parent's capacity to love, nurture, guide, support, and educate the children

- The children's cultural background

- Each parent's ability to support and encourage the children's relationship with the other parent (except in cases of domestic violence or child abuse)

- Any criminal history of either parent, either parent's significant other, or other members of the household

- The children's age, development, and temperament

- Any conflict between the parents

- Each parent's work schedule

- Any failure by either parent to financially support the children

- Each parent's moral character

- The potential for each parent to engage in abuse

- The children's physical, mental, religious, and social needs

- Any history of domestic violence or child abuse by either parent

- Any history of substance abuse by either parent

- Any intentional misleading of the courts or making of knowingly false allegations by either parent

- Continuity for the children

- The parents' capacity to cooperate

- Any history of child abduction by either parent

- Any recommendation by a guardian ad litem (an attorney appointed by the court to represent your children's interests) or custody evaluator

Most jurisdictions include a statement about "any other factors" and are clear that the factors are not pre-weighted (i.e., the judge can decide how much weight to allocate to any factor). Some jurisdictions also include a list of factors that should *not* be considered, such as either parent's gender or disability status (unless it impedes parenting capacity).

Be familiar with the specific factors listed in the statutes of the jurisdiction in which your case will be heard, and be prepared to discuss how your family dynamic can be understood in the context of these factors. In appendix A, we list the statutes in which you can find the specific BIC factors for your US state or district, Canadian province, or Canadian territory. (In Canada, the Federal Divorce Act RSC 1985, c.3 [2nd Suppl.] will also be relevant.) It is especially important that you note whether your statute includes a factor pertaining to each parent's supporting the children's relationship with the other parent. You can conduct an Internet search using the statute number and the phrase "best interest factors in" and then type in the name of your jurisdiction. That should bring you to the complete statute. Alternatively, you could ask your attorney for a list of the factors.

The next step is to prepare your evidence according to the BIC factors in the jurisdiction in which your case will be heard. Have one binder tab for each factor and include everything in that section that is relevant, such as letters and cards your children made for you extolling your many virtues, photographs of you and your children sharing loving moments, and appreciation awards from parent-teacher organizations. If you have no specific evidence to address a factor, then write a brief and bulleted list of points you could make about that topic, noting that you don't have documentary evidence to back up your points.

By the Five-Factor Model of Parental Alienation

In some legal motions, it may make sense to try to convince the judge that your children are rejecting you because of parental alienation, or your ex's undue influence. You, as the rejected parent, are claiming that your ex has influenced the children to unjustifiably reject you; that is, the children are rejecting you based not on your own behaviors and their history with you, but rather on your ex's actions and attitudes.

All children have issues and complaints about their parents; the question is whether your children's behavioral responses are proportionate to your normative flaws and whether your flaws are the primary cause of their rejection. You need to show that they are not.

Keep in mind that an important concept in your theory of the case pertains to the "primary causal factor" of your children's rejection. Your ex will present his own version of the situation, in which you are the cause of your children's rejection. To convince the judge that it is your ex, and not you, who is the *primary cause* of your children's disproportionate and unhealthy behavior—especially in light of the fact that your ex and the children will have legitimate complaints against you, because all parents are imperfect—it is essential that you present the judge with a complete and compelling alternative understanding of your family dynamics. We recommend the following five-factor model for doing so.

FACTOR 1: YOUR EX HAS INTENTIONALLY MISREPRESENTED YOU TO PROFESSIONALS

Your ex will be presenting a story to the judge that highlights your supposed flaws and the legitimacy of the children's complaints against you. To the extent that you can show the judge that your ex has exaggerated or manufactured these flaws and/or has provided misleading information about you to mental health and legal professionals, schools, neighbors, child protection services, and so on, you can demonstrate that the complaints against you are not real and do not account for the children's behavior toward you.

Intentionally misrepresenting you includes knowingly filing false allegations of child abuse or domestic violence against you; saying that you have a history of mental illness or violence when that is not true; telling the custody evaluator things about you that are patently false and/or egregious exaggerations; and making false statements about you under oath (in a deposition or on the stand). List each and every one of these false statements, indicate whether it is totally or partially false, and indicate which documentation and third-party affidavits or other evidence—if any—would corroborate this.

Another way to think about misrepresentations is that they represent excuses for your ex to undermine and interfere with your relationship with your children. If you can show that even your ex doesn't believe or really care about the alleged problems, you can undermine his theory of the case. One way to do that is by showing—as much as possible—that you have addressed the concerns in the past but no matter what you fix or change, your ex finds new issues to focus on to justify disrupting your relationship with your children. Thus, your ex pays lip service to wanting you to repair your relationship with your children but behaves in a way that indicates a lack of investment in the solution—for example, delaying the custody evaluation or undermining your efforts to reconcile with your children by canceling therapy appointments, by scheduling activities that conflict with therapy sessions and/or your parenting time, or by filing motions to have therapists removed from the case when there appears to be improvement.

FACTOR 2: YOU PREVIOUSLY HAD A POSITIVE RELATIONSHIP WITH YOUR CHILDREN

To feel comfortable granting your motion for access to your children (or denying your ex's motion to deny or limit your access to your children), the court will have to know that at one time, you and your children enjoyed a close and loving relationship and you played an active role in your children's lives. Your ex's version of events will most likely be that you were never involved or close with your children, or else that you were close but something changed. To refute this, you can assemble a collection of photos of you and your children sharing positive moments together at various ages and stages of their development. Second, you can present a list of the specific ways in which you were involved. Statements by "collateral contacts" (friends, family, coaches, teachers, etc.) that corroborate your presentation are essential. Here are examples of information you could share:

- I took the children to school three days a week when their mother worked early (approximately seven years).

- I picked the children up from school two days a week because their mother worked late on those days (approximately seven years).

- I cooked at least two family dinners every week.

- I oversaw the children's guitar lessons (ages five to nine).

- I did most of the food shopping for the family (at least seven years).

- I put our children to bed approximately three nights a week, as we alternated nights (approximately seven years).

Also helpful is any specific evidence of your involvement—for example, the program from the talent show in which you and your children performed together, a picture book you and your children wrote and illustrated together, scrapbooks you and your children made together, or a yearbook that lists you as someone who volunteered at school. Any verifiable evidence that you were as involved as you say you were would be helpful. This includes testimonials from parents, teachers, coaches, religious leaders, and the like, although many of these people may not want to get involved.

These anecdotal elements and examples are very important and potentially powerful. The key to getting people—in this case, the custody evaluator and the judge—to react emotionally to a story is in the details. Storytelling is a practiced art, and there is no better time to practice that art than in this context. Therefore, practice telling the story of a time when you were involved in your children's lives in a way that is compelling and emotional. The idea is to give the judge a clear and emotionally grounded view of you and your children, set in a specific time and place. If you can do this, it will be very difficult for your ex to convince the judge that you and your children did not have a close relationship.

Exercise 5.1: Telling the Story of Your Relationship with Your Children

Think about each of the following topics regarding your relationship with your children. You can jot down notes on a piece of paper (e.g., in a journal or notebook).

- The ten most loving moments with your children

- The most loving photographs of you and your children

- The ten most meaningful and heartfelt cards or letters your children have ever sent you

- The most significant milestones in your relationship with your children

- The best vacations and family trips you have taken with your children

- Ten things you have taught your children

- Ten things your children have taught you

Practice talking about these topics with your friends and family members until you are prepared to discuss them at a moment's notice. The more specific you can be, the better able you will be to discuss these topics with your attorney or in court to advance your case.

FACTOR 3: THERE HAS BEEN NO ABUSE OR NEGLECT BY YOU

If you have been guilty of child abuse, neglect, or domestic violence, then your children have a legitimate reason to be hurt, angry, or afraid of you (although the truth is that many abused children do not shun even the most abusive parent). Thus, it is essential that you demonstrate to the court's satisfaction that you have not engaged in these behaviors. Of course, proving a negative is not easy. The obvious place to start is the absence of an official finding by child protection services (i.e., that the complaint has not been verified). If there has never been an official claim against you, point that out to your attorney. Aside from that, you can try to show how your ex's statements that suggest that you have been abusive are incorrect or misleading.

FACTOR 4: YOUR EX HAS ENGAGED IN PARENTAL ALIENATION BEHAVIORS

Research on adults who as children were alienated from one of their parents, and research on parents who are currently dealing with alienation, has identified an extensive (but not exhaustive) list of parental behaviors that can foster children's unreasonable rejection of the other parent (Baker 2007; Baker and Darnall 2006):

- Bad-mouthing the other parent

- Telling the children that the other parent does not love them

- Creating the impression that the other parent is dangerous

105

- Limiting contact with the other parent

- Interfering with communication with the other parent

- Interfering with symbolic communication with the other parent

- Withholding love and approval

- Allowing and/or forcing the children to choose between their parents

- Confiding in the children

- Forcing the children to reject the other parent

- Asking the children to spy on the other parent

- Asking the children to keep secrets from the other parent

- Referring to the other parent by first name in front of the children

- Referring to a stepparent as "Mom" or "Dad"

- Withholding medical, social, or academic information from the other parent

- Changing the children's name to remove the other parent's association

- Undermining the other parent's authority

Following are examples of the types of evidence that indicate the presence of these behaviors. For each behavior, you can organize verifiable evidence and then follow that with notes that describe undocumented incidents—your attorney can decide whether they are worthy of including in your court materials and/or whether they can be a useful guide for deposing your ex or conducting a cross-examination.

Bad-mouthing. When it comes to your ex bad-mouthing you, documented examples are best. Include as evidence any letters, e-mails, or text messages between your ex and your children in which your ex is inflammatory or unnecessarily negative about you, or exaggerates your flaws and foibles. Affidavits by trusted and neutral third parties (e.g., teachers, coaches, religious leaders) that attest to the fact that your ex has made negative comments about you to your children are also useful, as are statements by your children (in writing, on tape, or to trusted third parties who will attest to it) that reveal that your ex has made negative statements about you. Statements to therapists, custody evaluators, or parenting coordinators can also be considered verifiable if they are included in these professionals' notes and records.

Undocumented examples of bad-mouthing include statements that you have personally overheard your ex make to your children about you. Also, statements your ex has made to you (e.g., "If you hadn't stolen the kids' college money, they wouldn't be so mad at you!") are clues as to the beliefs that your ex holds about you that are likely to be communicated to your children, whether directly or indirectly. In other words, your ex's strong beliefs are likely to be known and felt by your children, even if your ex claims not to share his views with them. Witnesses who can testify to your ex bad-mouthing you can be very compelling, helping take the issue out of the "he said/she said" realm.

Telling the children that you do not love them. As this is a specific form of bad-mouthing, the same principles apply here. Relevant documents include any e-mails or text messages from your ex that convey to the children that you are not a loving parent. Affidavits by trusted and neutral third parties (e.g., teachers, coaches, religious leaders) that attest to the fact that your ex made comments about you not loving them to the children are also useful, as are statements the children make—in writing, on tape, or to trusted third parties who will attest to it—such as "Daddy said that Mommy doesn't love us anymore since she married Kevin and has a new family of her own," that reveal that your ex has made negative statements about you. Any extended family members whom the children have shunned can also be credible witnesses and can raise the discourse above the level of "he said/she said."

Creating the impression that you are dangerous. This is another specific form of bad-mouthing. Relevant documents include any e-mails or text messages from your ex that convey to the children that you are not a safe parent for them to be with, such as a text message reminding the children to call if they feel scared or worried when they are with you. Affidavits by trusted and neutral third parties (e.g., teachers, coaches, religious leaders) or credible witnesses such as your extended family and friends that attest to the fact that your ex has suggested or stated to the children that you are not safe are also useful; so are statements by the children (in writing, on tape, or to trusted third parties who will attest to it), such as "Daddy said that Mommy doesn't drive safely and we shouldn't get in the car with her," that reveal that your ex has made statements about your not being safe. In one family of divorce, the favored parent (the mother) stipulated in the proposed court order that the daughter could never be alone in the car with the father, despite the fact that there had been no evidence of unsafe driving or unsafe behavior of any kind. Once that became the court order, however, the daughter most likely absorbed the belief that her father was unsafe. This is why it is so important not to make these kinds of concessions: because they can take on a life of their own in a child's mind. Your child may think, "There must be some reason the judge doesn't let me drive with Daddy anymore."

Limiting contact. Evidence of your ex limiting contact between you and your children includes any communication that reveals a lack of intent to comply with the parenting time schedule, such as "Sorry—Johnny will not be going with you today or any future Sundays because he now has soccer practice," and communication by your children regarding lack of intent to spend time with you, such as "Don't bother picking me up tomorrow—I am not going to your home this weekend." Video or audio recordings of your ex taking the children during your parenting time or discouraging you from spending time with them by saying things such as "You can try to pick them up, but I don't think they want to be with you" are also good evidence.

Obviously, documented statements by your ex will be most effective in court, as there can be no denying them. You may have e-mails or messages from your ex saying things like "I cannot believe that I had to miss the party to stay home and be with the kids since they didn't want to stay with you this weekend!" or "You have no right to be upset with me that I had to pick them up from your home. It's not my fault that you have so much trouble managing them." Another example of your ex's limiting contact is an emergency motion to cease contact for reasons that are, at best, weak. This would be particularly compelling evidence if your ex made repeated allegations against you despite no finding of their veracity. As noted earlier, family court judges may view a lack of investment in solutions (e.g., an inability to believe that you are not abusive, despite lack of validation by professionals) as a powerful indicator of the presence of alienation. Another example of your ex's limiting contact are requests that you voluntarily relinquish your parenting time in order to "honor" your child's voice. Such requests are especially suspect if your ex mentions honoring the child's voice only when the child is asking for *less* time with you. For example, in one family of divorce, the mother repeatedly tried to convince the father to voluntarily shorten his parenting time, based on a presumed desire on the part of the daughter. However, when the daughter expressed a desire to stay for the full visit with the father, the mother instructed the father to ask the daughter several times a day whether she was sure she wanted to stay with him.

Undocumented instances of limiting contact include any missed parenting time that you happen to not have proof of (proof being, for example, a statement by your ex that confirms that the children were with her when they should have been with you). It will help if you keep a calendar for the sole purpose of tracking your parenting time, indicating the dates and times your children are supposed to be with you. Whenever the children are not with you on your scheduled time, make a note of why. Consider routinely sending an e-mail to your ex asking for compliance and documenting noncompliance at the time of its occurrence, as this is strong evidence.

Interfering with communication. Compelling evidence of your ex's interfering with communication between you and your children includes any phone records that show that your calls are not being picked up when the children are with your ex, even though you are entitled to calls with them; audio recordings of you calling and being hung up on; your e-mails being returned or not read (this is possible to discern with some Internet service providers or through the "read-notify" service); and documentation of your repeated requests for the children's cell phone numbers met with either no response or a response that denies you the information (e.g., "You need to ask the children for their numbers.") Another example is your ex's dictating to you a very small and inconvenient window of time within which to make your court-ordered calls.

An example of unverifiable evidence of this behavior that may nonetheless be compelling if it correlates with other facts of the case is a log of the times you tried to reach your children and they did not answer (if for some reason this is not shown on your phone record) or did not come to the phone.

A corollary of this problem is when your ex inundates the children with texts and phone calls when they are with you—that is, when nonstop communications from your ex during your parenting time interfere with your children's relationship with you. As more and more children have begun to carry cell phones, this has become a serious issue in divorces. Verifiable evidence of such interference would come from your children's phone records.

Interfering with symbolic communication. Evidence of interfering with symbolic communication between you and your children includes any documented absence of photographs of you in your ex's home and indicators that your ex is not comfortable with or supportive of the children's talking about you. This may be difficult to document, unless a custody evaluator is looking for it or inadvertently mentions it in her report, saying something like "There are no pictures of Mrs. Jones in the father's home"; your child's therapist discusses this issue; or your child makes a witnessed statement such as "Mommy doesn't like us to look at pictures of Daddy. It upsets her."

Undocumented evidence of this behavior includes any statements by your children to you or other people that their other parent doesn't like them to talk about you or look at pictures of you. Other potential examples of interfering with symbolic communication are your children refusing to accept a picture of you to have at their other home and refusing to have their picture taken with you for no obvious or compelling reason, even though they are more than happy to have their photo taken with your ex.

Withholding love and approval. Evidence of your ex's withholding love and approval from the children could come from observations by neutral and trusted third parties, including the custody evaluator, and/or statements by the children that are witnessed by neutral third parties that your ex is not as loving and warm toward them if they express positive feelings about you. Perhaps your ex speaks in a colder tone of voice, snaps at your children, or turns his back and walks away in a huff.

Undocumented evidence of this behavior includes your personal observations that your ex behaves in a cold or standoffish manner with your children if they are near you and are being positive toward you (smiling at you, being affectionate, etc.). Again, these "undocumented" bits of evidence are much more credible if witnessed and attested to by "collateral contacts," even those who clearly favor you (e.g., your friends or family members).

Allowing/forcing the children to choose. Documents that demonstrate that your ex scheduled activities that conflict with your parenting time are a good example of your ex's creating situations in which the children feel that they should or have to choose your ex over you (as well as limiting your parenting time.) Communication with your ex might also reveal this behavior. For example, you may have an e-mail or letter from your ex stating that the children should be allowed to choose whether to visit you or suggesting that they would rather do something else on your parenting time and encouraging/pressuring you to go along with it.

Undocumented instances of this behavior include statements by your child to you such as "Daddy said I could stay with him next weekend and go fishing rather than be with you."

Confiding in the children. Documented instances of your ex's confiding in the children include any e-mails and texts from your ex to your children in which she shares personal information about you with them. Statements that your children have made to other people that indicate that they know things about you and/or about the custody dispute that they should not know also constitute evidence of confiding (as long as those people are willing to write affidavits on your behalf about these statements). If your children make statements to the custody evaluator, therapist, or child protection interviewer that reveal personal information about you or too much involvement in the details of the dispute, and these statements and observations appear in the final notes and/or report, those could be useful, especially if the children are observed using adult language and concepts. If your children reveal to the custody evaluator or a therapist that they are fully apprised of the ongoing dispute, and/or are overly concerned about and sympathetic to the favored parent's emotional struggles, suggesting parentification—for example, "Mommy trusts me enough to tell me what is going on"—and such a statement is included in the final report, that is indicative of confiding. Likewise, if your children have written letters to you pressuring you to make legal concessions, such as "I will come see you this weekend if you sign the great deal that Daddy made to you" or "We don't want to see you as long as you are trying to stop Mommy from moving," include these as evidence that your ex is confiding in your children. Some children come to a custody evaluator, therapy session, or child protection interview with a long list of grievances about the disfavored parent, which reflects too much and inappropriate information and is indicative of having been confided in.

Undocumented instances of this behavior include statements by the children to you, statements that you overhear them making to each other, or statements that they make to other people (who, for whatever reason, do not want to write an affidavit or otherwise get involved in your legal case) that reveal undue knowledge.

Forcing the children to reject you. Documents that are indicative of your ex's forcing the children to reject you include any letters, texts, or e-mails in which your children disinvite you to an important event (e.g., graduation ceremony, birthday party) or to school or extracurricular activities that you have a reasonable right to attend. They also include affidavits written by trusted people who heard the children make such statements, as well as any such statements that appear in a custody evaluator or therapist's report (e.g., "I told my mother that she shouldn't even bother coming to my birthday party"). Forcing the children to reject you is different from allowing or forcing the children to choose in that you are hearing the rejection directly from your children, as opposed to your ex's telling you about it (e.g., "Johnny said he would prefer if you didn't come to his school play this weekend.").

Asking the children to spy on you. Documentary evidence of your ex's asking the children to spy on you includes not only communications from your ex, but also communications from your children from which you can infer that they complied with such a request. Of course, probably neither your ex nor the children will use the term "spy," as that has negative connotations. Instead, your ex might tell the children, "Remember to let me know if you see a letter from the lawyer" or "Send me a photo of Dad's new car when you can"; or your children might say to your ex, "I tried to find the letter from the lawyer, but I didn't see it." Also, your children may make statements to the custody evaluator or therapist that reveal your ex has asked them to spy on you, and if such statements (or comments about such statements) are included in the evaluator or therapist's report, this can serve as evidence. If your ex submits information to the court (e.g., in a motion) that you can demonstrate your children likely obtained without your knowledge, such as by taking pictures of your home or copying documents that were in your home, this can also serve as evidence that your ex is colluding with the children to spy on you.

Undocumented instances of asking the children to spy on you include any time you found your children looking in your private papers or files in a way that strongly suggested to you that they were doing so at your ex's behest.

Asking the children to keep secrets from you. Evidence of your ex's asking the children to keep secrets from you includes any communication between your children and your ex suggesting an awareness of keeping something secret from you or withholding information about activities and events so that you miss them, such as "Remember not to say anything to your father about this." It also includes discussions between your children and your ex about matters that you have a reasonable right to know about, such as moving homes or schools, your ex's getting married or having a boyfriend or girlfriend move into the house, or the children taking up or stopping a hobby or an activity. For example, in one family of divorce, the mother and the son refused to tell the father which private high schools the son was applying to. Although it was the mother who initially refused to share the information, it was the son who chose to keep it a secret. The documentation, in a sense, is the sworn lack of knowledge on your part, coupled with your ex's refusal (in writing or under oath) to share the information. It can be inferred that your child was asked or persuaded to not share the information with you.

Other (undocumented) instances of keeping secrets include any statements by your children to you that reveal information that you should have had earlier, as well as any other time you found out something that they already knew about. For example, in one family of divorce, the father did not find out that the mother's boyfriend had moved into the home until he went into his former bedroom to retrieve something and saw the boyfriend's clothes hanging in the closet. It turned out that the children had known for several weeks already that the boyfriend was living in the house with them.

Referring to you by first name. Letters, e-mails, and texts to your children can serve as documented instances of your ex's referring to you by first name. For example, in one family of divorce, the mother directed the son to "Look at your father and say to him, 'Steve, I am frightened of you.'" This was clear evidence that the mother was encouraging (if not pressuring) the son to refer to his father by his first name. You might also use letters to you from your children in which they refer to you by first name. Statements appearing in the custody evaluator's or therapist's report or in investigative reports and school materials in which the children refer to you by your first name may also support the assertion that your ex is encouraging the children to refer to you by first name.

Undocumented instances of this behavior include any times when you overheard your ex refer to you by your first name, such as when you called on the phone to speak to your children or you came to the door to pick them up.

Referring to a stepparent as "Mom" or "Dad." Besides communication from your ex to your children, evidence of your ex's referring to a new spouse as "Mom"/"Dad" includes any forms (e.g., medical forms, school enrollment contracts, emergency contact forms) on which your ex listed the new spouse instead of you as parent. For example, in one family of divorce, the mother put the new husband's contact information in the space provided for the father and put the father's contact information in the space provided for the children's doctor (since he was, in fact, a dentist). Any e-mails, texts, or even cards from your children (if you can photograph or copy them) addressing your ex's new spouse as "Mom" or "Dad" would also constitute evidence.

Withholding medical, social, or academic information from you. Evidence of your ex's withholding important information from you includes any documents such as school enrollment forms, medical information forms, and sports team contact lists on which your ex did not include your contact information. Any form that includes a place for both parents' names and contact information should include your name and current contact information.

You can also include as unverified evidence an annotated list of every time that you missed an event of your child's because your ex did not inform you about it, every time that you showed up at the wrong time or place because your ex failed to notify you of a change (or include you on the form that would have allowed you to be notified), and every time your child informed you of a recent event that you could have attended but did not know about.

Changing your children's name to remove your association. In most instances, this would involve an informal name change, as opposed to going to court to effectuate a legal name change. Documents reflecting your ex's changing your children's name to remove your association include any letters written to your children, forms completed on behalf of your children, or statements in court or to the custody evaluator about your children in which your ex refers to your children by a different name than the one on their birth certificates (e.g., a mother referring to her children by her maiden name or using the last name of her new husband or significant other). Other examples include a different last name on the back of your children's jerseys, underneath their yearbook photos, on their school assignments, or in class lists.

Unverified evidence of this behavior includes hearing firsthand or secondhand that your children are now referring to themselves by a different name.

Undermining your authority. Documents pertaining to your ex's undermining your authority include communications in which your ex encourages the children to disregard your family decisions (e.g., "I don't care if Daddy said you have to do homework this weekend—I am taking you to see a show!") Also relevant is any communication from your ex that disparages your values, hobbies, or parental guidance.

Undocumented instances of this behavior include your ex's dropping off items at your doorstep that he knows you don't want the children to have, making disparaging comments about you, going out of his way to undo a lesson you are trying to teach, making up rules for what your children can and cannot do even at *your* house—for example, your child tells you (the mother), "Daddy says not to eat chocolate anymore, so I am not going to eat your pudding"—or making a decision with you about what your children can and cannot do and then going against it in a way that creates the appearance that you are the "bad guy."

FACTOR 5: THE CHILDREN EXHIBIT ALIENATION BEHAVIORS

Exposure to parental alienation behaviors can result in children's unwarranted rejection of the other parent. When children align themselves with the parent who is engaging in these behaviors and unjustifiably reject the other parent, they are likely to exhibit most, if not all, of the following behaviors, which differentiate them from children who have become estranged from a parent due to demonstrable abuse or neglect (Gardner 1998):

- A campaign of denigration

- Weak, frivolous, and absurd reasons for the denigration

- A lack of ambivalence toward both parents

- The "independent thinker" phenomenon

- A lack of guilt regarding poor treatment of the rejected parent

- Reflexive support for the favored parent

- Use of "borrowed scenarios"

- Animosity toward the rejected parent's friends and family

In each case, documentation would involve communications from your children to you and your extended family and friends; your children's statements about and actions toward you that a neutral and credible third party can attest to; and statements by your children that appear in therapists' and custody evaluators' progress notes or reports. Unverified instances would involve your children's actions and attitudes toward you for which there is no verifiable documentary evidence. It is important to remember that even though your children are engaging in hurtful behaviors, they are still only children and are behaving badly as a result of pressure and manipulation by your ex. They are not evil or malicious. Inside, they still want to love and be loved by both parents.

A campaign of denigration. A campaign of denigration is characterized by rude treatment of you, coupled with a denial of positive (or even neutral) experiences shared with you in the past and a willingness to broadcast these negative attitudes. Your children may behave in a hostile and disrespectful manner toward you; rewrite history to minimize your relationship and your contribution to their upbringing (e.g., seem unable to remember your attending certain events or being present on family vacations); and happily share their displeasure with anyone who will listen. Another sign that your children are on a campaign of denigration is an apparent lack of interest in improving their relationship with you. For example, when asked what might make things better, a typical alienated child will be unable to imagine what that would be and will seem uninterested in seeing the relationship improve. It is important to remember, of course, that your children have been put up to this behavior and that they are not evil or to blame.

Weak, frivolous, and absurd reasons for the denigration. When asked to provide a reason for their harsh and total rejection of you, your children may provide reasons that are disproportionate to the level of animosity they exhibit toward you and your extended family. For example, your children might complain that you do not let them nap on the couch, that the wooden floors in your house are scratched, or that you wear cowboy boots with skirts. In one family of divorce, the daughter complained that her mother took her to Disneyland too often, while also complaining that she did not do anything fun with her.

Absence of ambivalence toward either parent. Instances of this behavior can be found in statements, drawings, or stories by your children that portray you as all bad (i.e., evil, rotten, dirty, the devil) and your ex as all good (i.e., worshipped, a hero, an angel). Statements that indicate a total disregard of the need for or importance of you, such as "I don't need a father. My mother is all I need," are also telling. This kind of black-and-white thinking is unusual even for relatively young children and is not even seen in children who have a good reason to reject a parent (e.g., the parent abused them).

The "independent thinker" phenomenon. The hallmark of the "independent thinker" phenomenon is preemptive protectiveness toward the favored parent. For example, your children may go out of their way to assure you (and the custody evaluator, therapist, child protection interviewer, etc.) that their negativity toward you is in no way influenced by their other parent. A typical example is "Mom, don't even think of blaming Dad for this, but I have decided…."

A lack of guilt regarding poor treatment of you. While behaving in a rude and hurtful manner, your children may appear not to care about the pain they are inflicting on you. As a way to deflect blame and avoid guilt, they may claim that you "deserve" the poor treatment. Your children may be unable to acknowledge the pain and suffering their behavior causes you, even when a therapist or custody evaluator points it out. Inside, they may be feeling guilty, but they cannot admit that, even to themselves.

Reflexive support for your ex. Your children may side with your ex, no matter how absurd, illogical, or inconsistent her position is. They may display an absolute unwillingness to consider your point of view.

Use of "borrowed scenarios." Your children may use words, phrases, and concepts that they do not understand or cannot define and that you can readily trace to your ex's attitudes and beliefs. Your children may appear to have been coached, programmed, or brainwashed.

Spread of animosity to your friends and family. Your children may cut off beloved friends, neighbors, and family members based on their association with you. They may even abandon hobbies or interests if those hobbies or interests are associated with you; for example, your son, who loved playing soccer, will suddenly lose interest when you become a soccer coach.

Summary of the Five-Factor Model of Parental Alienation

When you can demonstrate to the court that you are a normative parent (that is, that while all children will naturally have some complaints and issues, yours have reacted disproportionately to the asserted issues and your parenting), and you can demonstrate the five factors noted, you can make the argument to the court that the family dysfunction is primarily the result of the favored parent controlling, manipulating, and confusing the children. Provided that your evidence and your theory of the case is explained properly to the court, and provided that the court perceives you in your testimony as a normative, empathic parent, you should be able to demonstrate that the primary causal factor for the children's rejection of you is not any problem with your parenting decisions or parenting style, even if these might be causes of some upset in your relationship with your child. After all, all parents have to set appropriate guidelines and boundaries, even in intact families. In demonstrating to the court that neither you nor your parenting is the primary causal factor for the family dysfunction you should be able to effectively negate the "hybrid" model of high-conflict custody disputes, in which the court does not intervene because it assigns blame for the dysfunction (to varying degrees) to both parents. This is essential for convincing the judge to hold your ex accountable for your children's alienated behavior.

Conclusion

Your attorney must be in possession of all the relevant facts and evidence pertaining to your case in order to advocate effectively for your rights in court. You must organize your evidence in a manner that will help your attorney easily access the essential facts. You can organize the evidence chronologically, by the best interest of the child (BIC) standards for the jurisdiction in which your case will be heard, or by the five-factor model of parental alienation. You will need to find the one that works for your attorney. It will also be helpful for you to provide your attorney with a fact sheet and a timeline of major family milestones.

CHAPTER 6

Preparing for a
Custody Evaluation

In some custody disputes, the family undergoes a custody evaluation. This involves a court-appointed mental health professional interviewing, assessing, and observing all members of your family to help the judge understand the family dynamics. The purpose of the evaluation is to determine the children's needs and to assess each parent's ability, willingness, interest, and aptitude to meet those specific needs. You can think of this as an in-depth study and investigation into your family and its members, and their relationship with each other. The purpose of the study is to assist the court in determining custody, visitation, and/or parenting arrangements that would be in the best interest of the children. Therefore, the evaluator will be looking closely at your parenting plan indicating your ability to meet the children's needs currently and under whatever changes you are asking for. In this chapter, we will explain the custody evaluation process and teach you how to avoid some major pitfalls while maximizing your opportunity to convey to the evaluator your version of the family dynamics.

Custody Evaluation Basics

A custody evaluation usually takes anywhere from a few weeks to a few months. Some can take much longer—over a year—and it is very important that you push for a deadline and timetable up front to prevent that from happening. (If you know that the judge will be responsible for setting the timetable, you can ask in your motion to appoint an evaluator that the judge limit how long it should take.) The custody evaluation is typically completed when the evaluator submits a written report to the court. Some evaluations include specific recommendations for what would be in the best interest of the children, and courts typically give a lot of weight to the evaluator's recommendations. Usually, it is the parent who is pleased with the recommendations who calls the evaluator into court to testify, but either side can do so. In some jurisdictions, both the attorneys and the parents have access to the evaluator's report; in others, only the attorneys have access to the report.

How a Custody Evaluator Is Appointed

Typically, in a disputed custody case, if one parent wants the involvement of a custody evaluator, the other side will resist. Therefore, the parent who wants an evaluation will file a motion requesting that the court appoint an evaluator. If the other side does not capitulate and sign a stipulated agreement, the judge may eventually begin the process of appointing one anyway.

In some jurisdictions, the court has a list of approved custody evaluators, and the judge will either select one himself or invite each side to suggest three names from the list. If there is one name that is suggested by both sides, that is most likely the person who will be appointed. (In other jurisdictions, such as Canada, there is no approved list, and each side offers a list of its recommended evaluators. It is important, as noted below, that the proposed expert have experience with your type of custody case—whether it involves one parent moving away, parental alienation, children with disabilities, or other issues.) The amount of time that is available for you to research the evaluators before making your suggestions varies. If you have a mental health consultant on your case, she can provide feedback about the approved evaluators and help you develop a strategy to try to get the one who is best suited to your case. It is also possible that your attorney is familiar with the suggested or approved evaluators and would recommend one over the others. If so, make sure that you understand why your attorney prefers this person. Otherwise, your attorney might recommend a psychologist with whom she has had good experiences, but not on cases involving the same issues as yours. If parental alienation is an issue in your case, keep in mind that some attorneys underestimate the power and uniqueness of the alienation dynamic, with the result that the evaluator they recommend fails to see how parental alienation truly affects the family. You can ask other parents in your area who are in high-conflict custody disputes whether they have had experience with the various approved evaluators.

Even though a custody evaluator is court appointed, the parents must pay the evaluator's fees, with the judge deciding what portion will be paid by each parent based on his understanding of their respective financial situations. Sometimes the costs are initially determined to be 50/50 and then reapportioned based on an analysis of each parent's financial status.

Types of Custody Evaluations

Sometimes, when ordering a custody evaluation, the judge will describe the specific type of evaluation he wants. The different types have different names in different jurisdictions. Some common names are parental responsibility evaluation, limited scope evaluation, and mini-evaluation or focused-issue evaluation. Each one involves coming to a conclusion about the family's functioning and the best interest of the children. What varies among them (other than their name) is whether they represent a complete, full-scale custody evaluation or whether the judge is asking for a more limited evaluation to answer a narrow question, such as "Should a parent be allowed to move away?" or "Has there been improvement since the last evaluation with respect to the children's relationship with one of the parents?" or "Have there been any changes in the family dynamics since the original evaluation report?" The evaluator will know what type of evaluation he is being hired to conduct, but you may need to find out from your attorney so that you can prepare.

What most, if not all, evaluations share is a focus on the best interest of the children (or at least the evaluator's understanding of that concept). You can refer to chapter 5 for a list of the factors that might be relevant in the jurisdiction in which your case will be heard. You may want to read the best interest of the child (BIC) statute for your jurisdiction (see the list in appendix A) so that you can find out which factors will be relevant in your evaluation.

The Custody Evaluator's Background and Credentials

Any licensed mental health professional (e.g., psychologist, social worker, psychiatrist) can conduct a custody evaluation. There is no specific "custody evaluator" license or credential. What qualifies someone to be a custody evaluator is specific training and experience in these types of evaluations, as well as knowledge of the law, although these qualifications are not always met.

The Custody Evaluator's Guidelines and Ethics

Each mental health profession (psychiatry, social work, psychology) has developed its own guidelines for conducting custody evaluations, as has the Association of Family and Conciliation Courts (AFCC). There are also dozens of textbooks about how to do custody evaluations. For example, the American Psychological Association's *Guidelines for Child Custody Evaluations in Family Law Proceedings* (2012) identifies fourteen principles for psychologists engaged in custody evaluation work, and an alternative list of principles is offered by the Association of Family and Conciliation

Courts (2006). There is ample overlap among these guidelines, but no two sets are identical. Moreover, they are just guidelines, as opposed to regulations. An evaluator who chooses to not follow any of these guidelines would not be behaving in an unethical or illegal manner (such behavior may be deemed incompetent, but not in a way that would necessarily be actionable by the relevant professional society). It may be helpful for you to be aware of the standards and guidelines relevant to your particular evaluator's profession, but the evaluator would probably not appreciate your giving him a list and/or grilling him on his understanding of them. However, if when the evaluation is over you believe that the evaluator has not followed the guidelines and that this has negatively affected the evaluation, you should discuss this with your attorney and mental health consultant, if you have one, because this can serve as the basis for a rebuttal to the evaluator's report.

Moreover, all the mental health professions (social work, psychiatry, psychology, etc.) have general ethical standards of practice, and it would probably be helpful if you were familiar with the standards to which your custody evaluator should be held. That way, you can know whether the evaluator violated any of these standards during the course of the evaluation, which could also be helpful in rebutting an unfavorable report.

Components of a Custody Evaluation: The Do's and Don'ts

A typical custody evaluation consists of the following steps:

1. An initial, office-based meeting with both parents (either jointly or separately) to review the ground rules and to discuss schedules and fees

2. Several office-based interviews with each parent (alone) to discuss his or her childhood, the marriage, parenting, and any concerns/issues about the other parent

3. Office-based personality and psychological assessments of each parent

4. Home-based or office-based observations of each parent with the children

5. Office-based interviews of the children (alone and in combination)

6. Telephone or in-person interviews with "collateral contacts," people who can attest to each parent's character

7. A review of documents provided to the evaluator by the parents and their attorneys

What follows is specific advice for handling each of these steps.

The Initial Meeting

A custody evaluation typically begins with each parent meeting (separately or together) with the evaluator in the evaluator's office, without the children present. The evaluator will let you know in advance whether you and your ex will be meeting separately or together. If a meeting with your ex would make you fear for your safety, you can always request separate meetings.

The purpose of the initial meeting is for the evaluator to review the ground rules and discuss the evaluation process with you, to answer any logistical questions, and to ask you to sign consent forms and necessary waivers. An evaluator needs a waiver to access the children's school records or to speak to a therapist (yours, your ex's, or the children's). You should sign these waivers promptly. The payment schedule is typically reviewed at this time as well.

Your demeanor will be noted by the custody evaluator, even during this preliminary meeting, so it is important to present yourself as a rational, focused, respectful, well-functioning person who respects the boundaries of the evaluator and the situation.

Therefore, don't drop by unexpectedly or make repeated calls to clarify minor details. Everything you do and say will be (or at least could be) noted by the evaluator and his staff. For example, if you are rude to the receptionist, it is likely that the evaluator will hear about it and form a negative impression of you.

It is acceptable for you to bring a list of questions to this first meeting, but it makes sense to let the custody evaluator explain things in his usual manner, without a lot of interruptions from you. It is important that you show deference to the evaluator, because misplaced enthusiasm or urgency to discuss your view of the case—essentially telling the evaluator what to think—will be poorly received. Once he has completed his initial presentation, you can ask further questions, but do so in a respectful manner and try to keep it to two to three targeted questions about your most pressing concerns. In addition, this initial meeting is not the time to discuss your concerns about your ex's behavior. If your ex is present for this meeting, be polite and refrain from rolling your eyes or trying to signal with your body language and facial expressions that you think everything he says is absurd and objectionable. If your ex says something that you do not agree with, you can politely say, "I have a different [perception/memory/understanding] of that [issue/event/experience]," but do not launch into your side of the story unless the evaluator invites you to do so.

Interviews with Each Parent to Discuss Childhood, Marriage, and Concerns

Early in the process, you will be invited to attend one or more one- to three-hour sessions with the custody evaluator without your ex or your children present. The purpose is for the evaluator to get to know you, your history, and your concerns. Many evaluation reports begin with lengthy descriptions of each parent's life history (where the parent was born and raised, the composition of his nuclear family, his education, major milestones in his life, relationships with his family, and the like), based on information supplied during these sessions. The evaluator is likely to ask you about your relationships with your parents and siblings when you were growing up, especially strengths and weaknesses in those relationships. Your transition to adulthood, such as what you did after high school and how supportive your parents were of your life choices, will be discussed as well. Certainly, the evaluator will ask you when and how you met your ex and to describe your early relationship—for example, why you fell in love with her, what you saw in her, and strengths and weaknesses of that relationship. Usually, the two parents have different versions of how they met and fell in love and what their early life together was like. And typically, the evaluator's report includes each parent's version.

When discussing your background and life history with the custody evaluator, it is important to stay focused. Answer the questions in a calm and focused manner, providing necessary details as requested. Make eye contact with the evaluator, and be honest about your own parents' limitations. It's to your advantage to show some ability to see them as flawed human beings with both good and bad qualities. The point is to show yourself to be a reasonable person, capable of nuanced thinking, who doesn't need to see other people in black-and-white terms. If you have unresolved issues with your parents, it is better to be honest about that than to pretend that you feel one way when you really feel another. Most likely, the evaluator will sense your hesitation. At the same time, do not confuse the setting for personal therapy. Avoid becoming so absorbed in describing the issues in your family of origin that you become overwhelmed with emotions and lose sight of the fact that you are in a custody evaluation.

During these initial discussions about your childhood and your relationship with your family, it is not helpful to try to convince the custody evaluator that you are a victim of your ex. You can ask when will you have the opportunity to share your co-parenting concerns, but you should refrain from focusing on that until the evaluator is ready.

Eventually, the custody evaluator should turn his attention to the problems in the marriage, the divorce, and the current custody arrangement. This is your chance to explain your concerns about your ex's behavior. Following are some things to keep in mind while airing your concerns.

YOUR EX HAS GOOD AND BAD QUALITIES

Do not insist (unless you really and truly believe it) that your ex has nothing of value to offer the children and has made no meaningful contribution to their lives and upbringing. Most likely, your ex has done *some* things well, and most likely the children have benefited in *some* fashion from their relationship with her. You will lose the evaluator's trust and respect if you claim that your ex has been completely out of the picture in terms of raising the children, never helped in any way, never spent time with the kids, and so forth. Be careful of exaggerating and of trying too hard to convince the evaluator that your ex is evil. You will be more effective if you use more moderate language. For example, it would be more helpful to your case to say:

> Their mom has been great in terms of putting the kids first and making sure that they have everything they need. She has been devoted to them and extremely attentive. When they were younger, she was very involved in their growth and development, especially when we had that problem with Sally's growth. She really went into action and found the best specialists. If it weren't for her, I don't know where we would be with that problem, which has thankfully resolved itself. I have also been a very involved parent. I stayed home with them one day a week and pretty much ran the show on Saturdays to give my wife a break. I would usually take the kids out for breakfast and then to the park to ride bikes. In the afternoons, we usually went bowling or ice skating. Over the years, I have been very involved in their sports activities, coaching Little League and soccer. I also try to stay involved in their schooling. I've often helped

with homework, especially math, and I have gone to most parent-teacher meetings. I think one of our problems is that my wife has been so wrapped up in the kids that she doesn't really have a life of her own and seems to have a hard time letting them go for their time with me. When I come to pick them up, she clings to them and looks really sad, and I think that makes it hard for them to have fun with me.

than to say:

Even though I worked full-time, I rearranged my whole schedule to take care of the kids. I did every bit as much as their mom did, if not more. She really has been a lousy mom since day one.

Of course, you should stick to the truth, whatever that may be, but the point is that a balanced approach is more believable than a blanket statement that your ex has done absolutely nothing good. No matter what your situation, come prepared with stories, examples, and evidence to back up your general statements. Try to paint a picture of life with the children prior to separation, replete with specific examples, so that the evaluator can identify with your experience (and therefore your position). Specific, concrete examples are much better than general statements in getting the evaluator to emotionally connect with you and your plight.

ORGANIZE YOUR CONCERNS

When you present your concerns about your ex, try to do it in an organized way, focusing on the main concerns rather than rambling or delving into too much detail. Some parents get wrapped up in telling a long and complicated story about the myriad of ways that they are concerned about the other parent's behavior, but too much detail and too much emotion can be tiresome for the custody evaluator. Rather than focusing too much on any one story or example, help the evaluator see a pattern. A single episode of bad behavior by your ex can always be excused, but a pattern is hard to ignore. Perhaps select half a dozen of your most pressing concerns and share those with the evaluator, letting him know that you have additional concerns that you would be happy to share as well. Provide the evaluator with specific examples of behaviors that are unlikely to be acceptable under any circumstances.

FOCUS ON THE EFFECT OF YOUR EX'S BEHAVIOR ON THE CHILDREN

Remember that the custody evaluator's job is to identify the best interest of the children, not the best interest of either parent (although you probably want to avoid using the phrase "best interest of the child," as it is overused and can appear to be self-serving). Before you meet with the evaluator, be clear in your own mind about how your ex's behavior has affected your children in terms of their well-being. If it helps you, make a list, focusing on any of the following areas that are of serious concern and in which you can provide specific examples:

- Decrease in level of happiness (e.g., your children are not as cheerful and relaxed as they used to be)

- Decrease in well-being (e.g., your children have more symptoms of stress, such as headaches, stomachaches, and fatigue than before)

- Increase in negative emotion (e.g., your children seem more sad, angry, frustrated, fearful, or cynical than before)

- Increase in negative behaviors (e.g., angry outbursts, hitting, tantrums, bullying, or lying)

- Increase in separation anxiety or insecurity (e.g., your children are less likely to spend time away from home and are more clingy and less interested in friendships than before)

- Decrease in confidence (e.g., your children appear to be more tentative and less sure of their ability to achieve their goals than before)

- Decrease in self-esteem (e.g., your children make more negative comments about themselves and their self-worth than before)

- Decrease in academic functioning (e.g., a decline in test scores, quality of homework, participation in class, or engagement in school subjects)

- Decrease in social activities and pleasure in social activities (e.g., your children receive fewer invitations to parties and events, experience more conflict with friends, or have given up hobbies and extracurricular activities)

Of course, you will need to be mindful that some of these changes in your children could be a result of the divorce or other factors, not a result of your ex's active influence. Your most pressing point should be that you see the changes and you are concerned.

Exercise 6.1: Judging the Effect of Your Ex's Behavior on the Children

On a piece of paper (e.g., in a journal or notebook), make a list of the issues you sense your children are experiencing and how those issues manifest. Be as specific as possible. Rather than saying, "My daughter isn't as interested in friendships as she used to be," for example, say "My daughter turned down an invitation to go with her best friend to a carnival, which is something she has always loved and would have jumped at the chance to do before."

HIGHLIGHT THE EFFECT OF YOUR EX'S BEHAVIOR ON THE CHILDREN'S RELATIONSHIP WITH YOU

Even if your children seem to be functioning well, you can highlight what you perceive to be the effect of your ex's behavior on the children's relationship with you, if you think that this is relevant. It is very important for you to acknowledge to the custody evaluator that although any decline in your relationship with your children could be due in part to your own parenting or the children's natural response to the divorce, you believe that, given the warm and loving relationship you had with your children prior to the divorce, your parenting and the divorce alone cannot adequately account for what is going on. It will be helpful if you share a story or two that shows just how extreme your children's behavior is to illustrate that what is going on is not a normative response to divorce. For example, in one family of divorce, the son came to visit the father carrying a fifty-pound duffel bag with everything he would need for the weekend (including water and sheets), because he had come to believe that the water in his father's home was contaminated and he could not sleep on the sheets, drink the water, or eat any food prepared in the home.

When discussing your concerns about the effect of your conflict with your ex on your children's relationship with you, make sure to demonstrate your appreciation of how difficult this must be for your children, rather than focusing on your outrage at your ex's manipulations. Keep your focus on your children's happiness and well-being. You can use exercise 6.2, which follows, to help you organize your areas of concern.

We suggest that you focus on the following four areas of your children's behavior:

- Resistance to contact and communication

    Examples may include your children's refusing to visit you altogether, frequently canceling or requesting shorter visits, asking to go to their other parent's home during your parenting time, refusing to engage with you on your parenting time (e.g., holing up in their bedroom and biding their time), answering monosyllabically when speaking with you, and being emotionally distant. Also included would be failing to answer your phone calls, or failing to respond to your texts or e-mails.

○ Rude behavior when with you

  Examples may include your children's calling you names, provoking you physically, accusing you of things you did not do, speaking to you in an arrogant manner, being unable to accept any feedback or criticism, lying to you, screaming in your face, or threatening to hurt you.

○ Preoccupation with approval from your ex

  Examples may include your children's paying attention only to your ex, not to you, when both of you are in the same space; frequently calling your ex to check in and seek approval; appearing worried about your ex being angry or disappointed, and excessively communicating with your ex (texting, etc.) when with you.

○ Making outlandish accusations that deny or distort your past relationship

  Examples may include your children's making statements that you were never involved and never loved them or that you wanted to hurt them, denying ever having fun or feeling close with you, and minimizing your importance (e.g., saying that it would be no big deal if you were out of their life forever).

Exercise 6.2: Changes in Your Children's Relationship with You

On a piece of paper (e.g., in a journal or notebook), make a list of the ways in which you believe that your children have changed in their responses to and relationship with you. Pay special attention to the four areas previously discussed, but make sure to include your own specific observations and experiences and to add any other items that are of concern to you. When compiling your list of concerns, make sure that you include only behaviors that you can offer specific examples of, and be as specific as possible.

BE HONEST ABOUT YOUR OWN LIMITATIONS AND FLAWS

It would be pointless to pretend that you are a perfect parent, because there is no such thing, and the custody evaluator will certainly see any such attempts in a negative light (she will think that you are psychologically unaware, immature, etc.). Make sure that you acknowledge and accept responsibility for your flaws but can also explain how, since these have never gotten in the way of your relationship with your children in the past, you do not really think that they are the real reason that your children are upset with you now.

If you believe that your ex is misrepresenting you to the children (and perhaps to others, such as teachers and coaches), make a list of character traits that you believe that your ex is falsely accusing you of having (e.g., you're angry, crazy, and irresponsible). Then select at least one or two specific examples of interactions between you and your children in which you displayed *opposite* character traits. For example, if you are being portrayed as impatient and easily frustrated, find an instance in which your patience was clearly on display, as was your frustration tolerance. Obviously, when you are with the custody evaluator, you should be careful not to display any negative qualities your ex is accusing you of having.

BE AWARE OF THE EXPERIENCE FROM THE CUSTODY EVALUATOR'S POINT OF VIEW

Try not to get so wrapped up in making your case that you become overly emotional (weeping uncontrollably, yelling, talking too intensely without pausing, etc.). As clinicians, custody evaluators are trained to make observations of a person's demeanor and presentation. They also are trained to be attuned to how they feel when in another person's presence and to infer something about that person from those feelings (e.g., *I am feeling tense because this person is so intense. I bet this is how the children feel when they are with their dad*). As a parent in a high-conflict custody dispute, you rightly have many strong emotions in response to your situation. You probably feel anger, frustration, helplessness, and sadness. But if you display such emotions in a meeting with the evaluator, the evaluator may wrongly assume that these intense feelings—whether intensely active, such as anger, or intensely passive, such as depression—are also present in your relationship with your children. Thus, you must be mindful of your body language, facial expressions, demeanor, eye contact, and ability to stay focused while with the evaluator.

Remember, if your ex is engaging in parental alienation, the custody evaluator will be hearing negative things about you not only from your ex, but also from your children. Because these negative things may have a grain of truth to them—your portrayal as cold and unloving may be drawn from your natural tendency to be reserved; your portrayal as hysterical may be drawn from your expressivity—during the interview the evaluator may find that the complaints he has heard about you seem to fit with his impression of you, strengthening the notion that your children have a legitimate reason to reject you. With this in mind, try to manage the impression you are making by being attuned to the evaluator. If the evaluator encourages you to elaborate on a story, then do so, but if the evaluator indicates impatience or lack of interest, then be aware of that and wind down what you are saying. You can also "check in" once in a while—for example: "Am I giving you too much detail? I know I can get wrapped up in these stories."

Expect the custody evaluator to ask you questions about your children—about their developmental histories, milestones, personalities, interests, and hobbies. Obviously, you should already know the answers, but it wouldn't hurt to make sure that you have really reflected on each child's unique personality in order to demonstrate your commitment to them and your investment in them. Think about who they are as individuals and what is most special about them. It would not make sense to either emphasize their pathology as damaged children or speak of them as being perfect. Try to be realistic and grounded in your actual experience and relationship with them over time. Also, if your relationship with your children has changed since the separation, try to illustrate the relationship you had with them before the separation, so as to create a clear contrast to the present. One of the biggest mistakes naïve custody evaluators make is to write a report that is a static snapshot and assumes that the current state of affairs is the way it has always been. This is devastating when parental alienation is involved. You must show the evaluator how much your relationship with your children has changed over time, rather than allowing the evaluator to conclude that there has always been strife and distance just because there is now.

Self-Care Tip

Because the stakes are high, a meeting with the custody evaluator can be a highly stressful experience. Try to get a good night's sleep the night before, know that the meeting may run long, and try to allow yourself some free time afterward so that you can refresh yourself and recover before having to engage in work or child care. Also, be mindful that the evaluator is not functioning in a therapeutic role. You may experience the evaluator as cold, dispassionate, and difficult to read, and it will be helpful if you are prepared for this.

Personality and Psychological Assessments of Each Parent

The custody evaluation will probably include an assessment of each parent's personality, mental health, and parenting style and capacity. You may be asked to take a number of standardized tests (paper-and-pencil measures in which you check off the response that best fits your beliefs and experiences). It is best to not try to "psych out" these tests, because they have built-in mechanisms for determining when someone is trying to create a false impression. Your best approach is to be honest in your responses and not try too hard to come off as perfect or without problems.

Your scores on these tests will be measured against cutoff scores for clinical issues such as depression and anxiety. However, at least one test that you are likely to take—the Minnesota Multiphasic Personality Inventory—uses a separate set of cutoff scores for people in high-conflict custody disputes, because high-conflict custody disputes are known to be so anxiety provoking (Bathurst, Gottfried, and Gottfried 1997). Knowing that should help you relax and be honest when completing the test and not worry that your anxiety related to your custody dispute will make you appear to have a mental illness.

Once you get the custody evaluator's report (if you have a chance to review it), if you believe that your scores on the various tests are not representative of your actual functioning, you can hire an expert with the purpose of reviewing and—if flaws are found in the evaluator's procedures or conclusions—rebutting the report. See chapter 7 for how to find such an expert.

If psychological testing "clears" your ex of serious mental illness, he may attempt to use these test results to demonstrate to the court that he is not acting unreasonably. However, you should know that although a psychological examination can rule out the presence of serious mental illness, it cannot rule out abusive behaviors or parental alienation. In other words, there is no psychological profile of "a manipulative ex-spouse." Although there may be some tendency for people with borderline personality disorder or narcissistic personality disorder to engage in vindictive, undermining, hostile, or malevolent behaviors in a custody dispute, there is no evidence (to date) that all people who act this way have one of these disorders or that all people with one of these disorders engage in this type of behavior. Thus, even if your ex is "cleared" of these disorders, that is not sufficient in and of itself to show that he is not engaging in the behaviors you are concerned about or that he is making the best choices for your children. Psychological reports have their place, but should not be given more weight than they deserve.

Observations of Each Parent with the Children

At some point in the custody evaluation, you will probably be asked to participate in one or more interactional sessions with your children. Obviously, the purpose is for the evaluator to observe your parenting style. If your ex will be bringing the children to these sessions, you can politely ask the evaluator whether it would be possible to request that your ex not wait in the waiting room. You have every reason to believe that your ex's mere presence on the other side of the wall could inhibit the children from engaging with you or being warm with you. Ideally, if you still have an ongoing relationship with your children, the appointment should be scheduled for a day when they are with you both before and after the observation so that they will not be subjected to any interrogation by your ex following the visit, as that could inhibit or affect them. If your ex does not agree to that, document this concern for the evaluator. If you have more than one child, and your relationship with each of them is dramatically different, and/or you worry that one child will inhibit one or more of the other children from warming up to you, you can request to be seen with the children separately.

Being Emotionally Present

The most important guideline to bear in mind during an interactional session is to be emotionally present for your children. This is not going to be easy if they are alienated, because they will most likely be distant and disengaged; hostile, rejecting, rude, and angry; and/or feigning fear. Any of these behaviors is likely to make you feel awkward, embarrassed, and angry. You will most likely want to turn to the custody evaluator and explain how aberrant this behavior is in light of your previous warm and loving relationship or say something like, "See how rude and nasty they have become?" However, any asides to the evaluator will take you away from being in the moment with your children. As painful as it may be, it is important that you try to stay present with them, even if they are ignoring or provoking you or behaving in an atypical manner. Keep your body and face oriented toward them, pay attention to what they do, speak to them in a kind and loving voice, tell them that you love and miss them, and show empathy for their plight by saying things like "This must be hard for you. You probably really don't want to be here right now."

You may be tempted to try to talk your children out of any feelings of anger or fear toward you. You might say, "This is ridiculous. You know I have never hurt you," or "How dare you accuse me of that? I have done no such thing," or "There is no need to be upset. Let's play checkers." To invalidate your children's feelings in this way would be a mistake, however. You might think your goal is to have a nice interaction with your children in front of the custody evaluator so that he can see for himself that you are not such a bad parent, but really what most likely matters to the evaluator is your response to your children—not so much what they do and say, but how you *are* with them. It would be better for you to just sit and be actively empathic and sensitively responsive to whatever feelings they express than force them to play a game to look good for the evaluator.

If your children do accuse you of terrible misdeeds (e.g., hitting their other parent, stealing their money), rather than ask them, "Who told you that?" or exclaim angrily, "How dare you accuse me of that?" it would be far better for your relationship with them if you commiserate with their feeling hurt and angry thinking that you would do those things. This is not to say that you should admit to something you did not do, but that from their point of view it could seem that these things happened and that could lead them to be hurt and angry. For example, you could say, "I can see why you would be so hurt and angry if you thought that I misspent your college funds. That would feel really bad to me if I thought my parent did that." If it is relevant, you can acknowledge how the situation lent itself to that conclusion on their part—for example, "I can see how you might think that I used your college funds when I bought the new house, but that is not the case." Likewise, if they express an idea or opinion that you don't agree with (e.g., related to the custody dispute), it is better to acknowledge their opinion and thank them for sharing it rather than try to talk them out of it. You might want to brush up on your active listening skills, discussed next.

Active Listening

Active listening is a technique for being present as a listener, aiming not just to hear but to understand what a speaker is saying. Even if you vehemently disagree with what someone is saying, it is possible (and important) for you to be curious and interested. Often, when your child says something to you that presents a problem—for your child or for you—you may find that rather than actually paying attention to what your child is saying, you are already anticipating how you are going to respond, especially to defend yourself. In doing so, however, you miss an opportunity to understand your child and show her that you care about her and her feelings. Active listening involves the following six elements:

- Nonverbal indications of paying deep attention (nodding your head, making eye contact, etc.)

- Brief verbalizations, such as "I see" or "Go on," to show the speaker that you are actively engaged in hearing

- Restating what the speaker is saying, to ensure accurate understanding

- Probing for more information

- Making an educated guess as to what the speaker is feeling, to fully understand the experience from the speaker's point of view

- Offering to problem solve

Practice active listening with a friend, to get the hang of it. You can even have your friend role-play your child being angry or fearful or distant, to help you develop your ability to stay attuned to your children when you feel as if they are making you look bad.

Highlighted Resource: *Co-parenting with a Toxic Ex*

In the book *Co-parenting with a Toxic Ex*, Amy Baker and Paul Fine (2014a) provide dozens of suggestions for when your children may be caught up in a loyalty conflict, like many children whose parents are in a high-conflict custody dispute. The book describes how to stay mindful and present while feeling anxious, how to use active listening to repair the wounds in your relationship with your children, and how to behave in a way that presents to your children a different reality than the false one their other parent is presenting.

Interviews of the Children Alone and in Combination

If your children are at least preschool age, it is likely that the custody evaluator will want to interview them separately (i.e., without you or your ex present). If you currently have no contact with your children, there will be no role for you to play in this part of the process. If you do have contact with your children, you should be aware that what you say to them about the interview and your demeanor when taking them to meet with the evaluator may shape their behavior in the interviews. Obviously, someone has to explain to the children that they will be interviewed. It might make sense to ask the evaluator her opinion of who should tell them and what to say. The main point to emphasize to your children will be that interviews are a way for the custody evaluator, who will help the judge decide about the parenting schedule, to get to know everyone in the family. As much as possible, alleviate or avoid creating any pressure on your children so that they do not feel responsible for the outcome of the evaluation. Reassure them that the most important thing is to tell the truth.

Discussion with "Collateral Contacts"

At one of your early sessions, you will probably be asked to bring in a list of "collateral contacts." These are people who can attest to your involvement (and, if relevant, your ex's lack of involvement) with your children, your attention to your children, and your loving care for your children. You might want to prepare a neatly typed list of these people's names, roles, and contact information (phone numbers and e-mail addresses). People to consider include:

- Your children's medical providers, including their pediatrician and dentist

- Your children's teachers, day care providers, and babysitters

- Your neighbors and your children's friends' parents

- Your friends and family members

  The evaluator will know that your friends and family members are bound to be positively biased toward you, but it is probably helpful to put them on the list anyway, to show that you have good relationships with them.

- Your mental health and medical providers

  You will have already signed waivers allowing the evaluator to contact these providers, so you may not need to put them on the list; and the evaluator may not give their impressions much weight anyway, because most therapists write nice letters for their clients. Nonetheless, you should include them, just to show that you believe that they would have good things to say about you. If you went to any couples or marital counseling and you believe that the counselor really had a handle on your ex, highlight this person's name.

You should let these people know your intention of sharing their contact information with the custody evaluator, but you should not tell them exactly what you want them to say. If they come off as rehearsed or scripted to the evaluator, he will probably not give their words much weight. He might even ask them what, if anything, you told them about the evaluation.

The Evidence Review

The custody evaluator will most likely be receptive to reviewing any documentary evidence that you want to submit. This will be discussed at the first information meeting. It is important that you find out what kinds of evidence the evaluator will want to see. For example, does the evaluator want (i.e., is the evaluator willing to read) a lengthy subjective narrative of your perception of the marriage and your ex, or does she prefer only "objective" documents such as court motions, verified e-mails, and school reports? Try to hear what she wants and then provide it to her in an orderly and coherent fashion. Avoid dropping off boxes of printed e-mails or loose papers. The evaluator will not appreciate the extra work of having to sort through and make sense of them. As with your attorney, you should keep a copy of whatever you give to the evaluator, in the same order and format, so that you and the evaluator can easily refer to the same document should the need arise. Your attorney might be able to advise you as to what evidence to submit, as might your mental health consultant, if you have one.

The Custody Evaluator's Report and Conclusions

Most custody evaluators submit a formal report to the court regarding their impressions and assessments of the individual family members and their relationships with each other. Some evaluations include specific recommendations with respect to parenting schedules and responsibilities and access to the children. The court is likely to give considerable weight to those recommendations.

Should the custody evaluator present misleading information and/or draw illogical conclusions, it might be wise to present the court with a rebuttal to the report. You can do this in at least two ways. First, you can hire an expert witness (see chapter 7) to explain how the information in the report actually reflects a different picture than the one portrayed by the evaluator—essentially, using the evaluator's own words against her. This would involve a substantive critique. Second, you can hire a custody evaluation expert or mental health consultant to rebut the evaluator's methodology by highlighting bias in the data collection process, flaws in the interpretation of test scores, and/or lack of competence in the approach used.

If you choose to rebut the evaluator's report, you should be mindful of whether the judge appears to hold the evaluator in high regard and whether your expert would appear to be biased. The more prestigious and competent your rebuttal expert, the better off you will be.

Conclusion

A custody evaluation is a very important part of a high-conflict custody dispute, because the courts tend to give a lot of weight to the evaluator's impressions and recommendations. At all times, you need to be mindful of the impression you are conveying to the evaluator. It will help if you take care to be respectful and appropriate, present your concerns in a thoughtful and organized way, and give a balanced and verifiable account of your history. If the evaluator nonetheless fails to understand your family dynamics as you do, you can always hire an expert to provide a credible critique of the evaluator's report (we will discuss this in the next chapter).

CHAPTER 7

Finding and Working with the Right Expert Witness

It is possible that you could benefit from bringing an expert witness onto your team. An expert (in this case, a mental health professional) could testify in court as to theoretical or research-based principles that are pertinent to your case that no other witness is qualified to testify about. For example, you might want an expert on move-aways (when one parent wants to move away with the children), parental alienation (when one parent is manipulating the children to unjustifiably reject the other parent), sexual abuse, or any other highly specialized topic, such as children with autism or other special needs. In this chapter, you will learn about different types of expert witnesses, the advantages and disadvantages of hiring an expert witness, and how to identify and interview potential expert witnesses.

Definition and Types of Expert Witnesses

Anyone who testifies in court is referred to as a witness. An expert witness is a professional who is "qualified as an expert by knowledge, skill, experience, training, or education" (*Federal Rules of Evidence* 2010, 14) and is believed to have specialized knowledge in a particular subject beyond that of the average person. This expert "may testify thereto in the form of an opinion or otherwise, if (1) the testimony is based upon sufficient facts or data, (2) the testimony is the product of reliable principles and methods, and (3) the witness has applied the principles and methods reliably to the facts of the case" (ibid.) An expert witness is different from a fact witness—like a coach who overheard your ex berate the children, a pediatrician who can testify that your ex denigrated you in front of the children—who is not an expert but is testifying based on facts that he has personal knowledge of.

Another important distinction is that some expert witnesses testify based on their general knowledge, training, and experience about a subject (e.g., sexual abuse) without being familiar with the details of the case; other experts offer testimony regarding the details of a particular case (in this case, your family dynamics). An example of the former would be an expert on false accusations of sexual abuse who educates the court about why and how often this occurs in custody disputes; an example of the latter would be an expert on sexual abuse who reviewed the video of a child protection services investigation interview with your son and can comment as to the flaws in the interview process.

It is also possible for a mental health professional who is not a clinician to provide expert testimony about high-conflict custody dynamics based on a document review, but only under certain conditions and with certain caveats in place. First, the expert witness must be completely clear with the client and his attorney that he is not a clinician and will not be conducting assessments, interviews, testing, or observations of family members. Second, the expert must be clear in his language in any reports or oral testimony that he is not diagnosing individuals. The appropriate language to use would be to say that an individual is behaving in a manner that is consistent with alienation/loyalty conflicts, or undermining or interfering behaviors, or whatever the issue at hand is. If the client and attorney agree that this is acceptable, then the expert witness can proceed.

As we mention throughout this book, it is also sometimes advisable to hire a mental health consultant, someone who does not testify in court but provides you with "behind-the-scenes" consultation in terms of selecting an attorney, reviewing the work of other experts, helping you understand legal strategy, and interacting with other professionals and systems. Any expert you hire in that capacity would not be a witness; therefore, you are not obligated to inform the other side that you retained such an expert, and should this expert prepare written documents for you, those documents are not subject to "discovery" (meaning you are not obligated to share them with the other side). Because we already discussed this type of expert in chapter 4, in this chapter we will focus on retaining an expert for the purposes of educating the court and testifying in court as an expert witness.

Advantages and Disadvantages of Hiring an Expert Witness

You might think that—aside from costs—there are only upsides to having an expert witness on your team. However, that is not necessarily true. You should understand the potential advantages and disadvantages so that you can make an informed decision whether or not to hire an expert witness. Of course, this is a decision you will make in collaboration with your attorney and mental health consultant (if you have one), and in the end you should follow their advice, unless you have a very good reason not to. For example, if they strongly advise you against hiring an expert witness in general, a particular type of expert witness, or a particular expert witness, it would be unwise to not at least consider that advice, especially if it is based on their assessment of the judge's receptivity to experts or to a particular expert witness. If the judge tends to frown on expert witnesses, you could actually harm the judge's perception of you if you hire one.

Advantages

There are certainly some advantages to hiring an expert witness. First, when your attorney submits the name of your expert witness to the court (which must be done by a certain number of days prior to the first day of the hearing, along with that person's CV and sometimes a list of topics to be addressed in the testimony, known as interrogatories), you are alerting the other side that you take the case very seriously and are bringing to bear all the resources at your disposal. If your expert witness has name recognition or appears to be an important person in the field, the other side may agree to a settlement rather than proceed. The other side may also choose to settle rather than proceed if prior to the hearing your expert witness submits a report (as is required in certain jurisdictions) that is compelling and powerful.

The second advantage is that you will have someone who knows the field and the topic of hostile custody disputes, parental alienation, or false accusations inside out and who can explain to the judge your issues of concern in a clear and compelling manner. Your expert witness can address any potential arguments against your position better than you can and will hopefully be more convincing to the judge. Keep in mind that the family court system is biased in favor of the status quo. For example, in order to be considered, any motion to "modify" the current court order must show there has been a substantial change of circumstance. Consequently, it is generally incumbent upon the parent arguing for a change to present an overwhelming case in order to overcome this bias. Any of the criticisms raised by opposing counsel could be enough to sway the judge to not intervene (e.g., to not impose sanctions on your ex, to not enforce visitation, to not order reunification, to not transfer custody). If you are the parent arguing for change, an expert witness may effectively discredit any attempts to confuse the judge about the validity of your claims.

Disadvantages

Unfortunately, there are also some potential downsides to bringing an expert witness to your team. The first is the expense and the risk that the effort may not be worth it. The court could decide not to allow your expert to testify, your expert could have a bad day in court, or the judge could be unreceptive to your expert's opinions and testimony. Worse yet, your expert witness may actually damage your case by allowing herself to make concessions under cross-examination that contribute to the judge's favoring your ex on an important point. In some courts, simply having an expert witness might appear as if you are trying to push your weight around with a "hired gun." This is why it is essential that you involve your attorney in the decision regarding whether to hire an expert witness.

Because you (and your attorney)—not the court—select the expert witness, and because you are paying this person, there is the obvious potential downside that your expert witness will be perceived as biased in your favor. If opposing counsel can find ways to demonstrate that your expert is in fact biased in your favor, this person will be of little value to you on the stand. Throughout this chapter, we highlight ways to eliminate or at least minimize the potential for bias, as well as the appearance of bias, in your expert witness.

It is also possible that informing the other side that you have hired an expert witness will trigger a decision on their part to hire an expert witness as well. For every expert who is willing to educate the court about the issues in your high-conflict custody case, there is at least one who is willing to testify as to why your concerns aren't valid. It is possible that the other expert's testimony will cancel out your expert's testimony and you will have gone to the expense for nothing. Of course, you cannot know this in advance, so if your ex hires an expert witness to discredit your expert witness, all is not necessarily lost. For every criticism of your expert's testimony, there is likely a good response. Therefore, it is essential that the expert you hire as a witness be familiar with the specific issues in your case and know how to respond in advance to any criticisms the other side is likely to raise in court.

Before you raise the issue of hiring an expert witness with your attorney, prepare a list of pros and cons and share them with your attorney (and mental health consultant, if you have one). You may also want to ask your attorney whether she routinely works with expert witnesses and if not, why not. Your attorney may have her own list of pros and cons.

If you and your attorney agree that an expert witness makes sense for your case, the next step is to determine whether you want an expert who can educate the court in general or one who can review and comment on the specifics of your case. You may want a witness who can educate the court if a clinician has already evaluated the family and made a conclusion that you are in agreement with and you want the expert to testify about why the court should take that clinician's conclusions seriously. For example, if the custody evaluator concluded that your children are alienated, it may help to have an expert testify about how damaging alienation is to children. On the other hand, if no such clinical opinion exists, then an expert could review the documents and—if she agrees—testify as to how alienation is present in your case.

Finding Prospective Expert Witnesses

Thanks to the Internet, you can probably identify many potential expert witnesses across the country (and the world) who have experience with the specific issues or situation that you are dealing with. The first thing you should know is that not everyone who claims to be an expert on a particular issue actually is one. It is important that the expert you retain be able to pass what is known as the *voir dire* phase of the hearing. This is the process during which your attorney demonstrates to the court that the proposed expert witness is in fact a qualified expert by reviewing in direct examination the person's educational background, achievements, credentials, publications, and so on. During voir dire, the opposing counsel has an opportunity to attack the expert's credibility, education, and experience. This cross-examination may be extremely aggressive, so it is wise to know how the potential expert witness has done in this area. You can find this out by discussing with the expert whether he ever hasn't been admitted as an expert by the courts. See below for how to interview a potential expert. Imagine how embarrassing and damaging it would be for you in court if the judge dismissed your proposed expert witness as lacking sufficient expertise—in addition, you would probably still have to pay that person's fees. Thus, you want to ensure that your expert has not only "expertise" (meaning a high degree of knowledge), but also the kinds of credentials that the court would deem acceptable. This would rule out most people whose primary claim to expertise is running an online support group for parents in high-conflict custody disputes, as well as a parent who has taken it upon herself to become educated about the problem or who self-published a memoir about her experiences in court. Typically, expert witnesses have advanced degrees from prestigious academic institutions; have published books or at least some scholarly articles on high-conflict custody disputes or topics such as false accusations, parental alienation, noncompliance with custody agreements, children in custody conflicts, and the effects of divorce on children; and have provided workshops and trainings to mental health and legal professionals.

It would be ideal if your potential expert witness also had courtroom experience, especially in the jurisdiction in which your case will be heard. Not all academics and clinicians who might be bona fide experts in their field are competent and compelling on the stand. You want someone who not only has a firm grasp of the concepts, but also can clearly and compellingly articulate and explain the issues for the judge. You also need someone who knows how to handle herself on the stand so that she can respond to the cross-examination in a way that does not undo all the good that she contributed by her direct examination. This is a completely different skill set than being a good clinician or a good researcher. The best way to tell how effective someone will be on the stand (other than observing her actually on the stand) is to have your mental health consultant or attorney thoroughly interview her. Your attorney may decline, in which case (if you do not have a mental health consultant) *you* will be undertaking this task.

Interviewing Prospective Expert Witnesses

Once you have identified a potential expert witness, the next step is to determine whether she is the right one for your case. As previously noted, it is typically best if your attorney takes on the responsibility for finding and interviewing potential expert witnesses, as this will eliminate any appearance that your expert witness is biased in your favor—the judge will assume that your attorney acted professionally in this task and did not attempt to sway or bias the expert. However, if these tasks fall to you, there are a few things to be mindful of from the start when conducting an interview.

First, you should not begin the interview by launching into a long explanation of your family situation. Start by explaining that you would like to discuss the possibility of the expert's being a witness in an upcoming case you have in family court. Tell the expert your name and the name of your ex and your respective attorneys. That way, you can rule out any conflict of interest. Also, tell the expert what jurisdiction the case will be heard in and the proposed dates of the hearing. If the place and/or dates will be a problem for the expert, you might as well know this up front so that you can rule this person out.

Second, you should not share the details of your case, no matter how tempted you feel to do so. There is good reason for this, whether you hire the expert to testify in general about a dynamic affecting your family or you hire her to testify specifically about your case: once she is under cross-examination, it is quite likely that opposing counsel will try to make it appear as if you and the expert engaged in lengthy conversations about the case and that this information (and perhaps any warm feelings shared between you) shaped her testimony in court. If you are looking to have an expert testify regarding your specific case, you will provide her with the appropriate information later, in the form of evidence, once you have retained her.

If you are speaking with a nationally recognized expert whose books you have read and whose videos you have watched, you may feel compelled to share your story and perhaps even seek some advice about how to handle your situation. However, it is important that you maintain a professional and limited relationship with the expert in order to maximize her effectiveness on the stand and to allow her to maintain a position of objectivity. Most mental health professionals are bound by standards for their profession that forbid what is known as a "dual relationship," which means that with a few exceptions, the expert cannot function in more than one capacity for any client. She cannot function as your coach or therapist while also being your expert witness. Knowing this should help you maintain your focus on this person's potential to be an expert witness in your case. As noted above, the primary reason to limit how much of your story you share with the expert during the initial discussion is that it protects her from accusations of bias stemming from extended contact and communication about the case. If opposing counsel can create the impression that your expert witness is biased, then the judge will be less inclined to listen to what she has to say.

A sample introduction to the expert may go something like this: "I am calling to discuss the possibility that you could be an expert witness on an upcoming case I have in family court in the state of New Jersey in Bergen County, scheduled for June 15. My name is Mary Smith, and my attorney's name is Carol Sherman. My ex's name is Jacob Sanders, and his attorney is Denise Atkins. Is there any reason, based on what I have just told you, that you would not be able to accept the case?" If the expert says that there is no reason, then the next thing to ask is whether she has any "inclusion criteria" (elements of a case that must be present for her to accept the case) or "exclusion criteria" (elements of a case that must be absent for her to accept the case). An example of an exclusion criterion is that you have been found guilty of child abuse. Some experts refrain from testifying in such a case. Assuming that nothing in your case disqualifies the expert from working with you,

you should proceed to ask about her courtroom experience, her approach to dealing with the various issues in your case, and her contract and fees.

Prior Experience

Ask about the number of similar cases the expert has worked on and how many have gone to court in which she has testified. You also want to know whether she has ever testified in the jurisdiction in which your case will be heard (judges care about this) and whether she has ever undergone what is known as a Frye, Daubert, or Mohan challenge, in which the judge is asked to rule on the scientific merit of a theory about which the expert will be testifying. Passing such a hearing demonstrates a high level of competence. (The names Frye, Daubert, and Mohan refer to various court decisions about what scientific theories and experts are admissible.) It would be worthwhile to ask the expert to provide references: an attorney and a client (not necessarily for the same case) for whom she has served as an expert witness. Also, ask whether your attorney can speak to her (at no cost) to determine whether she is a good fit for your case. It may be tempting to ask how many successes she has had in court, but the outcomes of legal proceedings are determined by many factors, and it would be unfair to hold a bad outcome against an expert witness, just as it would be unwise to credit her with a good one. Also, outcomes are not always clearly good or bad, even to the client. Sometimes, it takes time to see how things will pan out (e.g., will the other parent comply with the terms, will the children come around in therapy?).

In summary, the following set of questions can help you assess whether the expert would pass the voir dire. Jot down the answers so that you can make comparisons when interviewing multiple experts.

- Does the person have the requisite educational degree (PhD, MD, LCSW)?

- Is the person currently employed in a relevant field?

- Does the person have the requisite expertise in the issue you're dealing with (e.g., one parent wanting to move away, allegations of abuse, parental alienation)?

- Is the person a clinician, a researcher, or both?

- Has the person ever *not* qualified as an expert in court?

- How many cases has the person testified in?

- Can the person provide you with a referral?

- How many cases in your state, province, or territory has the person testified in?

- Has the person ever participated in a Frye, Daubert, or Mohan challenge?

Demeanor

When interviewing a potential expert witness, you probably want to pay as much attention to the tone and style as to the substance of his responses. Obviously, you want the expert to have cogent, authoritative, and thoughtful responses to the issues you raise, but, just as importantly, you want to get a sense that the expert has a pleasant and appealing manner. Judges are human, and, as such, they are susceptible to the same subliminal influences as the rest of us. If an expert mumbles, uses jargon, rambles, or is supercilious, you probably would not want to hire him—or you should know that if you do hire him, he has some work to do on his demeanor on the stand. The ideal witness is authoritative (i.e., has a good grasp of the knowledge base) while being pleasant—not too colloquial and friendly, but not standoffish or snobbish either—and professional.

Beyond the obvious areas of education, experience, and publication record, the most important quality in an expert witness is his ability to be persuasive and personable while remaining objective. Expert witnesses often believe that it is beneficial to show hostility toward the other side; in actuality, this will alienate the judge, who will perceive them as biased and lacking objectivity. Keep in mind that the best expert witnesses maintain the posture of being objective and not "in the client's pocket."

In summary, you need to determine whether the expert maintains a professional demeanor throughout the conversation; whether the expert demonstrates an ability to explain his thoughts and ideas in a cogent and authoritative manner; and whether the expert demonstrates a pleasant manner (not too distant or formal, not condescending or pedantic).

Contract/Fees

Some expert witnesses ask the client to sign a formal contract. If there is a contract, make sure to have your attorney (and mental health consultant) review it with you before you sign. If there is no contract, make sure that you understand the fees, what services will be provided (e.g., document review, written report), and other basic issues such as refund policy (a refund would be expected if the retainer/replenishment was more than the fees charged). You can enlarge the following worksheet (or download it from http://www.newharbinger.com/30734) and use it to help you get answers to these questions.

Worksheet 7.1: Questions to Ask a Prospective Expert Witness About Fees

Hourly Fees

What is the hourly rate?

_____

Does this rate apply to all activities (reviewing documents, writing, traveling, testifying)?

_____

Is there a flat rate for out-of-town work?

_____

Is there a discount for extended out-of-town trips?

_____

Travel Expenses

If airfare is required, who books the flight?

_____

Does the expert fly first class or coach?

_____

Who books the hotel?

_____

What incidental expenses are to be reimbursed (taxi to hotel, parking at airport, meals, etc.)?

_____

Payment Structure

How much of a retainer is required?

_____

How are replenishments handled (e.g., invoiced on a regular basis)?

_____

How are payments made (e.g., wire transfer, check)?

_____

When is payment expected? (Some experts expect to be paid in full prior to testifying.)

_____

Refunds

Are refunds given?

_____

How is the refund request made, and is the refund in full or minus time spent?

_____

Review these terms with your attorney, who will know what is normal and customary in the area where you live. If you accept the terms, put them in writing in an e-mail to the expert and ask her to confirm that you and she are in agreement about them so that you will have a paper trail.

Self-Care Tip

Interviewing prospective expert witnesses can be exhausting and is likely to bring up many painful and intense feelings about your situation and the desperation you feel to be understood, validated, and helped. You may have an intense desire to share your story and to get help and insight. In order to avoid the frustrating experience of the expert interrupting your story to say that such a discussion could compromise her objectivity, try to remind yourself of your goals in speaking with an expert. Also, there is nothing preventing you from seeking social and emotional support from other venues. You can seek expert assistance from other experts in the field in terms of counseling, coaching, therapy, social support, and the like.

If you do become flooded with feelings while interviewing potential expert witnesses, try to do some caretaking of yourself once you are off the phone—take a bath, take a walk, do some deep breathing, use positive self-talk to heal and nurture yourself, or call a friend to debrief and process the experience. Remind yourself that you are only human and that what you are going through is extremely painful and challenging.

Preparing Evidence for Your Expert Witness

If you want your expert to educate the court about your case in general, then no evidence review is necessary, and, in fact—as noted above—it is helpful if the expert does not know any of the specifics of the case.

However, if you want your expert to testify about the specifics of your case, typically he will base his opinion and testimony on the documents you provide as evidence. (Your ex will probably not agree to participate in an assessment by your expert, nor will he allow the expert to interview or observe the children.) Ideally, before conducting a full document review, he will conduct an initial review to determine whether he believes that your concerns are valid (taking into account the limits of a document review process). You would not want to pay the expert to conduct a full document review that does not support your position, and you would obviously not want to submit such a report to the court. Thus, you want to ask the expert first to review the documents sufficiently to obtain a sense of whether your concerns are valid, but not so thoroughly as to cost you the price of a full, in-depth review.

It will be helpful if you are thorough, objective, and organized in the presentation of your evidence to the expert. You (or your attorney or mental health consultant) can use the same binder/section system described in chapter 5, except that you should be careful to supply only objective documents requiring little in the way of elaboration, explanation, and interpretation, unless instructed otherwise. In court, the expert will need to justify her conclusions that your concerns are valid, and your evidence must stand on its own. Your expert cannot, for example, justify interpreting a certain e-mail as being indicative of interference by having had you explain the necessary background information. Her conclusions must be based on the verifiable facts of the case, not filtered through your interpretation. It would be viewed as highly unprofessional for your expert witness to take you at your word on any matter, because objectivity would require hearing your ex's side of the story as well. Because it is highly unlikely that your ex would participate in a discussion with your expert witness, you must refrain as much as possible from sharing your interpretation of events with your expert witness. Try to remind yourself that such actions will discredit your expert witness with the judge.

Along the same lines, it is very important that you share "the good, the bad, and the ugly" with your expert witness and not try to shape her impression by withholding negative information about yourself. If your expert does not know all the facts, then her conclusions will not be valid, and this will surely be revealed during cross-examination. Imagine how damaging it would be for your expert witness to have opposing counsel show her a document that could alter her conclusions. She will appear to be biased (for not eliciting the document from you), and you will appear to have engaged in underhanded and misleading tactics. What you want is for your expert witness to share your understanding of your family—even after knowing everything there is to know about you and your family. Do not be surprised if, as she reviews the evidence, your expert keeps pressing you for more documents, to ensure that she has everything she needs to make an informed judgment. It may be helpful for you to ask yourself what your ex believes is going on with the family and what is the basis for those beliefs, then try to find objective documents that challenge that belief so that your expert can testify that she considered those possibilities and ruled them out.

Because you are paying your expert witness by the hour, you will save time and money by giving her the evidence that she wants in the order that she wants it. Ask her how she would like the evidence organized (by best interest of the child standards, by the five-factor model of parental alienation, chronologically, or some other way).

Once you deliver the evidence to your expert witness, ask her how long it will be before you receive a response, what format the response will be in, and to whom the response will be delivered (you or your attorney). Should she believe, after the initial review, that your position is supported, ask her how long it will take her to write a report, if a report is required, and how soon she will be ready to testify (this will help you plan). Because jurisdictions vary as to the form of expert documents (letters, reports, etc.), make sure that your attorney informs your expert witness of the rules of evidence for the jurisdiction in which your case will be heard. One argument for proceeding without a report (if a report is not required) is that a report opens the "playbook" for the other side. If a report is required, the review of drafts can be subject to discovery (not protected by privilege). Your expert should discuss these issues with your attorney (or mental health consultant) prior to preparing a report so that the expert is aware of the constraints he is bound by.

Conclusion

There are advantages and disadvantages to hiring an expert witness. You should make this decision, like all major decisions regarding your case, in consultation with your attorney and your mental health consultant, if you have one.

Expert witnesses vary as to their credentials, their knowledge of issues related to high-conflict custody cases, and their skill on the witness stand. When interviewing prospective experts, focus on the person's education, current and past professional positions, scholarly and academic publications, prior experience in court, and any relevant mental health and legal trainings the person has conducted. In addition to impressive credentials, any prospective expert should have experience on the stand testifying about the topics relevant to your case.

CHAPTER 8

Addressing False
Allegations of Child Abuse
and Domestic Violence

As a parent in a high-conflict custody battle, if you haven't experienced some negative "branding" designed to influence your children's perception of you, consider yourself very fortunate. If you have, or you are worried that you might, this chapter is for you.

When your ex negatively brands you, your children's perception of you as a safe and loving parent is eroded and replaced with a perception of you as unsafe, unloving, and unavailable so that eventually everything about you is viewed in this light. All your choices, characteristics, and qualities are considered somehow unsatisfactory and worthy of criticism if not contempt. You—your very essence—is seen to be the problem, and thus everything you do and say is portrayed as inadequate.

Many parents in high-conflict custody disputes denigrate the other parent not only to the children, but also to the community. Teachers, coaches, religious leaders, your neighbors, your ex's neighbors, your children's friends' parents, and the staff at your children's doctors' offices may all be receiving the message that you are a bad and dangerous person who does not love his children or that you are selfish for obstructing the children's wishes (to move away, to change the parenting schedule, to stop or start specialized services, etc.). If you are a woman, you might be described as hysterical and crazy. If you are a man, you might be described as having anger problems or being a bully or a monster. This vilification eventually could involve the engagement of child protection services, domestic violence services, and the police. Whether or not government services are involved, your "brand" in your community can be eroded and a false image of you can take its place. In a sense, the involvement of services—as damaging as that can be—is secondary to the corruption of your image in your children's hearts and minds. If the community within which your children live accepts the false view of you propagated by your ex, then this view will seem more accurate in your children's minds. When the "world" adopts the view of you that your ex is conveying to your children, it tips the scale away from "he said/she said" to "Dad must be right— Mom really is crazy. Everyone thinks so." What your children are not aware of is that "everyone thinks so" *because* your ex has spread negative messages about you around the community. They just see that their teachers, coaches, and so on agree with your ex that you are a bad person and a bad parent who does not really love them.

If you walk into a PTO meeting and feel as if everyone is looking at you with animosity, fear, or contempt, you will probably not want to come to another PTO meeting. If the receptionist at your children's pediatrician's office gives you a weird look, you may be tempted to skip the next visit. If you show up at your child's soccer games and all the other parents huddle around your ex in a show of support for her and contempt for you, you might not attend the next game. However, if you withdraw and avoid the places where your ex has bad-mouthed you and shaped others' impressions and opinions of you, you will inadvertently confirm whatever negative messages they have heard about you. If you fail to show up at the doctor's office, the staff will think, "Mr. Jones is right—this mother really doesn't care about her kids. She hardly ever comes to the office visits." Your absence will only confirm the view of you that they already hold. In a sense, your ex has primed them to believe that you are a bad parent so that the moment you do something that fits that idea, it locks into place as a fact. Likewise, if you arrive late for your child's soccer game because your ex didn't tell you the start time was moved up, and you lose your temper, shouting at your ex, "What do you mean, the time was changed?! Do you know how hard I worked to rearrange my schedule to come to this game? And now I find out that the soccer schedule changed and no one told me!" surely the coach and any parents who hear you will have their negative view of you confirmed. This is in part due to a cognitive process known as *confirmatory bias*, in which people favor information (i.e., pay more attention to it, give more weight to it) that is consistent with their preexisting views. Be aware that anyone who is on board with a negative image of you may be listed by your ex as a "collateral contact" (see chapter 6) or even serve as a witness in a hearing. Remember that third-party accounts hold weight for the judge, so they can be quite damaging to you.

Another reason to not avoid these places and events despite feeling unwanted and/or uncomfortable is that you will miss opportunities to share important events in your children's lives, which can erode the bond between you. Your children will feel hurt and angry (and rightly so) if you put your feelings of discomfort above your desire to support them and share in their lives. To have a relationship with your children is to share moments together, to be there in the moment (as opposed to hearing about it later) to cheer them on, to show your pride in them when they try and when they succeed, and to encourage them should they feel disappointed that they did not achieve a goal. Sometimes you may opt to avoid an event at which your ex will be present because you wish to spare your children some discomfort. This, however, reinforces your ex's portrayal of you as unloving. The fewer experiences that you share with your children, the weaker the bond between you will be and the more susceptible your children will be to your ex's influence.

Being criticized for who you are as opposed to for what you have done, as happens with negative "branding," can evoke a deep sense of shame and helplessness. It may make you want to hide or disappear. However, despite feeling deeply uncomfortable, you must not give in to the shame and embarrassment by avoiding the important places and events in your children's lives. Instead, you must be keenly aware of the impression you are making on others and try to correct yourself if you are behaving in a manner that could contribute to the negative view of you that your ex has painted. Your dilemma concerns how to be authentic and present while also being aware of how others perceive you, moment to moment. There is no simple way to do this. The best you can do is be aware of the messages your ex is spreading about you and try not to confirm them, while not being so consumed with your impression that you fail to be emotionally and mentally present for your children (and others with whom you are interacting). Try to be attuned to the vibe of the group (whether at a PTO meeting, at the doctor's office, or in your child's classroom if you are volunteering) and their experience of you.

The following exercise will help you identify the various people whom you suspect your ex has bad-mouthed you to so that you can not only be especially aware of your interactions with these people, but also identify strategies for managing their impressions of you.

Exercise 8.1: Combating Your Vilification in the Community

On a piece of paper (e.g., in a journal or notebook), create three columns. In the first column, write the name of each person in the community whom you believe is being exposed to negative messages about you (e.g., the coach, a teacher, a neighbor). In the second column, next to each name, indicate what the message is. Then, in the third column, indicate what you can do to counter the message without denigrating your ex (because it could backfire by turning that person off, and because what you say could be repeated back to your ex and used against you in court). The more specific your plan is, the better.

For example, if your ex is telling the pediatrician that you don't provide proper nutrition for your children, rather than approaching the pediatrician with the intent to bad-mouth your ex (e.g., "I can't believe he is spreading lies about me!") or with the goal of enlisting the pediatrician on your side (e.g., "You will testify in court that I am a good parent, right?"), you would benefit by showing genuine interest in the topic, such as by saying: "I'm under the impression that my ex might have concerns about the meals I provide for my daughter. Can I review some nutritional guidelines with you to make sure that I'm following them so that I can reassure my ex that our daughter is well cared for?"

Although you do not want to reinforce your ex's false messages about you, you also should not overlook opportunities to improve yourself as a person and a parent. Thus, if you believe that people in the community are not responding warmly to you, you can always start by looking at yourself to see whether you are doing anything that might be contributing to the problem. Do not assume that every criticism of you (by your children or by others) is solely the result of your ex bad-mouthing you—if you do, you may close yourself off from constructive feedback and opportunities to improve and enhance your relationships.

Allegations of Abuse

Not all custody disputes involve formal allegations of abuse or neglect—meaning those made through child protection services—and certainly not all allegations of abuse or neglect are false. However, bearing in mind that your ex might falsely make a formal allegation (if this has not happened already), there are some steps you can take to protect yourself.

To begin with, we suggest that you refrain from corporal punishment of any kind (e.g., spanking, pinching, hitting, swatting, slapping) in order to eliminate the possibility that you could inflict injury resulting in a physical abuse claim being filed against you. Also avoid grabbing your child or restraining your child physically, unless it is absolutely necessary in response to a safety concern. Any time that you are feeling angry at your child, make sure to avoid physical contact. For example, if your child is having a temper tantrum and you are at the end of your rope, do not angrily pick him up and carry him brusquely to a time-out corner, because you may frighten or inadvertently injure him. Stay calm and in control of your emotions. If your child hits you or provokes you physically, you should withdraw a few steps and deal with the matter verbally.

To protect yourself from allegations of sexual abuse, refrain from being naked in front of your children, sleeping under the covers with them (or even lying on the bed with them, unless you are fully clothed), bathing with them, washing their private parts (after a certain age), kissing them on the mouth, allowing or enabling them to watch R-rated movies (e.g., by not having parental controls activated), or having any kind of pornography in the house (kids have a way of finding things). Make sure to always knock before entering bedrooms and bathrooms and wait a moment before entering in order to respect your children's privacy. You also might want to be very mindful about any kind of sexual teasing, horseplay, wrestling, and suggestive language. In other words, any type of verbal or physical contact can be misconstrued, so be very clear in your boundaries and behavior.

The best advice currently available for avoiding allegations of sexual abuse by children is meant for teachers (e.g., avoid all physical contact, do not spend time alone with a student, do not show physical affection). Unfortunately, were you to follow these rules with your children, you would be denying them the warmth, love, and affection that they require from their parents. Thus, the best advice is not to limit *all* physical affection but to avoid behaviors that are not necessary for showing affection (kissing on the mouth, nudity, etc.) and be mindful of any situation that could be misconstrued by your ex. It is also especially important for you to guard against your children's being able to access sexually explicit material on any electronic device (computers, smart phones, tablets, pads, etc.).

Another piece of advice is to document in a journal any events that might be construed as questionable. For example, if you accidentally walk into the bathroom while your child is in the shower, make a note of the date, the precise time that the event began and ended, and what was said and seen. That way, should anyone accuse you in relation to this incident, you can refer to your notes rather than rely on your memory. You might also want to document what you were doing just prior to and following the event, to show how short a time it spanned.

To protect yourself from allegations of neglect or inadequate supervision, make sure that you do not leave your children alone in the house or car (even for a short time) unless they are well above the age when they can handle this. Ask the police, ask child protection services, check online, and ask your friends who are also parents to find out what age is considered acceptable. Do not keep alcohol, prescription drugs, or any poisonous substances within your children's reach. Make sure that your children do not unnecessarily show up late for or miss school, fail to complete their homework, or miss their vaccinations and annual physical exams. Do not let your children forgo a car seat until they are the proper age and height (this varies by jurisdiction) or forgo wearing a helmet while riding a bike or skateboarding. In other words, be very clear about your responsibilities as a parent and make sure that you are fulfilling them, to the exact letter of the law. This will not completely protect you, but it will certainly help.

Should your ex or your child make false allegations of sexual abuse against you, you should be very concerned. Any kind of official finding against you can haunt you for life. If you are found guilty of (or you plead guilty to) sexual abuse or misconduct against your children, you may be placed on a national registry, which could affect your standing in your community and your ability to get a job. It will certainly be an influential factor in the minds of the judge, the custody evaluator, and any other legal and mental health professionals in your family's lives. The most important thing for you to do, therefore, is not sign anything without consulting your attorney. Should your attorney encourage you to plead guilty to something you did not do, get a second opinion. Some attorneys minimize the importance and effect of pleading guilty and may urge you to just sign something that says you engaged in sexual misconduct to "make this whole thing go away," but the only thing that goes away when you confess to something you did not do is your innocence in the court's and your family members' eyes. It seems likely that an admission of guilt would only make your life exponentially more difficult with respect to custody and access to your children. As we have noted, the courts are biased toward protecting children, and so the judge and the custody evaluator are likely to give considerable weight to a finding of sexual abuse.

Unfortunately, sexual abuse investigations can be error prone. There is often room for subjective interpretation on the part of the investigator. Although there is ongoing debate about the proportion of false allegations both in general and within the context of custody disputes, what matters is the finding in your particular case. A mental health consultant can help prepare you for your interview with the investigator, and afterward it probably makes sense for you to hire a sexual abuse expert to review the procedures used in the investigation. Most, if not all, jurisdictions require that the investigator's interview with the child be video recorded, and your attorney can request a copy of the video on your behalf. The expert can then review the video to determine whether proper interview procedures were used.

Finding an Expert to Review Videos of Sexual Abuse Interviews

As with any kind of expert, you can begin your search by asking your attorney for recommendations or looking on the Internet. Because not all experts are created equal, it is essential that you screen out those who would be unlikely to pass the voir dire process should your case proceed to court. That is, opposing counsel will try to disqualify your expert from testifying by demonstrating that he does not have the credentials to qualify as an expert. You should carefully interview prospective experts about their education (What is the highest degree the person has, from what institution is the degree, what is the degree in, is the person a licensed clinician, what is the license in), training (clinical experience conducting sexual abuse interviews, research experience studying sexual abuse interview protocols, other relevant training), prestige and credibility (national recognition in the field of sexual abuse interviews, authoring of any peer-reviewed publications on the topic, acceptance as an expert in the field of sexual abuse interviewing, number of times the person has testified on this topic, any trainings conducted on the topic of sexual abuse interviewing), and familiarity with sexual abuse interviews in the jurisdiction in which your case will be heard.

Ideally, as noted throughout the book, your attorney or mental health consultant should be the one conducting these screenings, to avoid any appearance of bias on the part of the expert. Whether you retain an expert or review the videos with your attorney, here are some questions to consider when determining whether the investigation was conducted properly:

- Is a structured protocol mandatory for interviewing children in the jurisdiction in which your case will be heard? If so, which one?

- Was a structured interview protocol used with your children?

- Which interview protocol was used?

- Can you get a copy of the interview protocol?

- Were the recommended components included in the actual interview?

  - A rapport-building phase in which the interviewer and children make small talk about topics unrelated to the purpose of the visit

- A discussion of the distinction between a lie and the truth, with an opportunity for the children to demonstrate their understanding

- A discussion of the interviewer's fallibility, with the children practicing correcting the interviewer

- A discussion of the fact that the children may not know the answer and to say "I don't know" rather than guess, with opportunities for them to practice this

- A discussion of a neutral event, to establish a baseline of the children's typical responses

- A discussion of the event that led to the interview (beginning with open-ended questions and proceeding along a continuum to more focused questions)

- Closure

- Were the following errors made?

  - Suggestive or leading questions (supplying information or creating expectations for specific answers)

  - Improper reinforcement (e.g., "You can have a cookie if you tell me more about...")

  - Asking the same question multiple times in order to get the "right" answer

  - Invoking fantasy, pretend, or hypothetical situations

- Was the interviewer's demeanor improper?

  - Did the interviewer appear to use social cues that signaled what the "right" answer was?

  - Did the interviewer appear to be biased (e.g., praising your ex, making faces when the children spoke of you)

  - Did the interviewer appear to lack healthy skepticism?

- Did the children lack credibility?

  - Was their use of language to describe the event incongruent with their developmental level?

  - Was the quantity and quality of details they provided not believable? For example, did they provide lots of details about the baseline event but speak only in general terms about the sexual abuse event, or, conversely, did they supply many more details about the sexual abuse event than the baseline event, using language that was not consistent with their general vocabulary level?

  - Was their sexual knowledge not in excess of what would be expected based on their developmental level?

  - Did their story change in significant aspects over time and from one telling to the next?

  - Did their story lack plausible descriptions of your alleged behavior, especially regarding threats and coercion?

  - Did their story lack plausibility with respect to how and when the abuse took place?

- Was a full assessment conducted, or just a child interview? A full assessment includes the following elements:

  - Interview of non-accused parent

  - Interview of accused parent

  - Medical exam of child

  - Interview of witnesses, if any

If you believe that your children were improperly interviewed and/or you were improperly investigated, it is important that you consult your attorney and/or mental health consultant on the best way to bring that information to the judge's attention. If child protection services made a finding against you, you might be entitled to appeal the finding. Consult with your attorney about the advantages and disadvantages of doing so.

Temporary Restraining Orders

As noted above, child protection and domestic violence services and investigation systems are biased in favor of protecting children and victims of abuse. This is a good thing. As a society, we want to protect children and other vulnerable populations. At the same time, it is vital that you understand that this bias can be easily exploited. The first thing you should know is that your ex can file a motion seeking a temporary restraining order (TRO) against you without your knowledge (this is called an ex parte order). You are not guaranteed due process in this context. The first you hear of a TRO might be when you receive notice that it has been granted. Usually, you will have an opportunity to file an "answer" and to prepare for a hearing at which your ex will ask for the TRO to be converted into a permanent restraining order (RO). When you receive notice of a TRO, you should do a few things:

- Make sure that your attorney is informed of the TRO immediately.

- Read the TRO carefully and make sure you know what constraints have been placed on you.

   For example, you are probably forbidden from being within a specified distance of your ex (and perhaps your children). Make sure that you do not violate that rule. For example, make sure that when you go to pick your children up for your parenting time, you do not inadvertently violate the order by being closer to your ex than is allowed in the order. Any violation of the order will increase the likelihood that it will become permanent.

● Maintain your cool at all times.

If you have an angry outburst at your ex—whether in person, on the phone, or by text—you can be certain that evidence of your behavior will appear in court and be used against you.

Too many attorneys minimize the importance of the TRO hearing and encourage the client to plead down or sign a stipulated agreement to "make this go away." Such attorneys may be unscrupulous, lazy, or uninformed, as the ramifications of signing a TRO may be far-reaching. For example, in some jurisdictions, the guilty plea/finding is entered in a searchable database that anyone can access. It could appear on any background checks and could be the reason you are turned down by a prospective boss or landlord. In addition, should you violate the terms of the TRO (even by accident), you could be arrested and face criminal charges. Also, there are some experts who will not testify on your behalf if you have pled guilty to domestic violence—even if you say that you signed the order just to "make it go away." You should not agree to attend anger management classes either unless you really believe that you need to, because—again—it brands you as dangerous and confirms your ex's poisonous messages about you.

A hearing for a restraining order is a very serious event in your life. Thus, should your attorney encourage you to "let it go" (i.e., not attend the hearing) or sign something, get a second opinion. You are permitted to bring full documentary evidence, along with an attorney to plead your case, to the hearing. Simply showing up prepared to defend yourself may make the judge think twice.

Supervised Visitation

In some cases, when children refuse visitation with a parent, the judge will order the children and parent to have visitation at a supervised visitation center. This could be because the judge has concerns about your children's safety or because the judge believes that the supervised setting will be more conducive to a visit (i.e., your ex will be more inclined to produce the children, and the children will be more likely to behave themselves). Some parents are so eager to see their children again after a prolonged absence that they will agree right away to supervised visits. Before you do the same, you should be clear that this can brand you in yet more ways that are harmful to your case and your relationship with your children in the long run. You probably should consider declining supervised visitation, because to accept the condition of supervision could reinforce for your children the idea that you have done something wrong. However, it is understood that you may decide to proceed with supervised visitation based on your desire to see your children, even under these circumstances. The key is to propose alternatives, such as transitions at neutral supervised locations or visits that are accompanied by a friend or family member. It is also important to include a time at which the supervision will no longer be needed and regular access will resume.

Another factor to consider is that a supervision center, as an entirely artificial environment, is not very conducive to the creation of loving, warm moments. The staff members who provide the supervision are not necessarily licensed mental health professionals who understand the dynamics of high-conflict custody disputes. If they take a disliking to you or observe your children rejecting you, they may write unflattering progress notes, which can end up in front of the judge, making it harder for you to progress to unsupervised visits. In other words, the staff members have power without necessarily the training and the knowledge to properly use that power. Again, confirmatory bias can make you look bad.

If you do proceed with supervised visits, here are some pointers. First, be aware at all times of the impression you are making on others, and avoid any behaviors that could create even the slightest appearance of abuse or neglect. For example, do not use physical discipline (i.e., punishment, restraints), pay attention to your children and their emotional and physical needs, and respect their personal boundaries. In addition, avoid spending time with your children away from supervision (e.g., in the bathroom) or otherwise out of view. Do not denigrate your ex to the children, and do not engage in any discussion of legal or financial matters. Also, avoid intense displays of emotion (weeping, scolding, etc.), because anything that seems unusual may be included in a report that could reflect badly on you. Make sure to arrive on time, depart on time, and respect all the center's rules, and if you are unclear about something (e.g., whether you can bring food, give your children gifts, watch a movie together with your children), ask in a respectful manner and follow the guidelines to the letter. If you roll your eyes and act as if the rules are stupid, you will be insulting the people who work there, which might come back to hurt you.

Supervised visitation is a one-down position for you. It is highly likely that your supervisors/monitors will assume that you must have done something to deserve being supervised. As frustrating as that may be, it would not be appropriate to engage them in discussions about your case, why you think you were railroaded by the courts, or how your ex is brainwashing your children. That could be awkward for them, as it will appear as if you are trying to convince them of something that they have no way of knowing for themselves. You will have to accept that these people will start from an assumption of your likely guilt. The best way to bring them around is to be respectful toward them and their guidelines and behave in a loving and appropriate manner with your children.

Conclusion

When the "world" adopts the view of you that your ex is conveying to the children, the children will be more ready to adopt this view as well. This may then become their prevailing view of you, tainting your relationship with them as it is continually reinforced by others. Therefore, a very important task for you as a parent in a high-conflict custody dispute is to not confirm your ex's negative messages about you, either to your children or to anyone in their social network or community, because if negative messages about you take hold in the community and are internalized by your children, they can be very hard to negate.

Your ex's vilification of you can spread to government agencies, such as the police, domestic violence services, and child protection services. You can proactively protect yourself—to a degree—from false charges of abuse or neglect. Do not plead guilty or no contest to anything you did not do, and if your attorney urges you to do so to "make it go away," you should probably get a second opinion. It is essential that you come to your temporary restraining order (TRO) hearing prepared with witnesses, evidence, and an attorney. You may be able to hire an expert to determine whether the investigation was conducted properly, and, if it was not, you can file an appeal. At all times, you must be aware of the impression you are creating and the perception others are forming about you and your relationship with your children.

CHAPTER 9

What to Ask for in Court

In most custody conflicts, there comes a time to present your proposed remedy—whether in a motion or cross-motion, under direct examination, to the custody evaluator, or through an expert (if the expert is permitted to express an opinion regarding what should happen). If you are trying to prevent your ex from doing something that you don't agree with, such as moving away or stopping/starting a service for your child, your proposed remedy should state exactly what you want (e.g., your ex is not allowed to move away, your ex is not allowed to sign the children up for therapy without your permission, your ex is not allowed to cease special educational services without your permission).

However, if your relationship with your children has been compromised, then your remedy should be focused on some combination of the following:

- Having your ex stop doing things that you believe are undermining and interfering in your relationship with your children while beginning to proactively support that relationship

- Repairing your relationship with your children

In this chapter, we will present some current thinking about how to achieve those two goals.

Repairing Your Relationship with Your Children: Eight Elements of a Solution Regardless of Custody

Whether you seek full custody (with eventual phase-in of contact with your ex) or something else, you can request the following elements to help your family to heal and move forward. You and your attorney can decide which ones to ask for and the proper language to use when doing so. The underlying assumption with all of these is that your ex has interfered with and/or undermined your relationship with your children.

Element 1: Authority Figures Provide a Clear and Unambiguous Expectation That the Children Will Repair Their Relationship with You

It is important that your children be informed that the legal and mental health professionals involved believe that what you are asking for in court (assuming that it involves some increase in or enforcement of your parenting time) is what will be best for them and that everyone has their best interest at heart and has clear expectations for how they will behave. They need to know that the weight of the court is behind the plan and that it is not simply a matter of you versus their other parent. They also need to be told that both parents are on the same page with respect to the current plan. Therefore, the following points should be written into the final order and/or conveyed directly to your children by the judge, your attorney, or your children's therapist:

- It is understood that they love and are loved by both parents, who have good points and bad points.

- Sometimes, parents have difficulty sharing their children during a divorce, and they do things that make the children feel that they have to side with one parent over the other. This does not make either parent a bad person.

- ○ Sometimes, children of divorce feel angry with the parent they think is responsible for ending the marriage. These feelings do not make the children bad. However, it is not healthy for children to side against a parent with whom they had a good relationship before the divorce. The court believes that this is what has happened in your family, and everyone involved (including your ex, ideally) is concerned that the children harbor untrue thoughts and unfair feelings toward you. The time has come to fix this problem. Their other parent is going to start being supportive of their relationship with you, and if that does not happen, their other parent will have to spend less time with them. They are going to be respectful and kind to both parents.

Your children need to hear from a neutral third party (i.e., not just you or your ex) that the plan to repair their relationship with you has been endorsed by the court based on a careful and thoughtful assessment of what will be in *their* best interests.

Element 2: Each Parent Will Refrain from Interfering and Undermining Behaviors

Both you and your ex should be provided with a list of behaviors and attitudes to refrain from engaging in (these behaviors are listed in chapter 5), with examples of each one. The last item on the list should be "Anything else that undermines the children's relationship with the other parent." This prohibition will extend to each parent's family members and friends and includes every form of communication (phone calls, text messages, e-mail, etc.), with immediate and automatic sanctions for any and all violations. (As the court only has jurisdiction over the parties to the case, the parent and not his/her family and friends can be sanctioned by the court. The parents can be made directly responsible for shielding the children from the negative views of their extended family members and friends, although those third parties can be directly controlled only through a restraining order.)

It may be even more beneficial if each item in the list is worded affirmatively rather than negatively. For example, rather than stating that the parents should refrain from denigrating each other, the list could state that the parents should speak positively about each other. This would make it easier for the parents to bring evidence that they have complied with the order, since it is easier to prove a positive than a negative.

Element 3: The Favored Parent Will Admit His Role in the Problem

The favored parent (your ex) should be instructed to write a letter to the children in which he acknowledges that he has done and said things that could have made it hard for them to love and trust you. The letter should make it clear that he has encouraged them to believe things that are not true, such as:

- That he is all good and that you are all bad (that you are dangerous, incompetent, unloving, etc.)

- That he loves them more than you do

- That you are not a good and loving parent

- That it was appropriate for him to engage them in discussions about parenting plans and court activities and to believe that they should be able to decide whether and when to visit with you

Your ex should give the letter to the children's therapist, who will read it to them if and when it is appropriate to do so. Your ex should reinforce these ideas in all ongoing interactions with the children, including but not limited to during therapy sessions that he might be invited to attend.

Element 4: Each Parent Will Refrain from Negative Communication with the Other Parent and Actively Promote the Children's Relationship with the Other Parent

Both you and your ex should be instructed to refrain from making derogatory and unsupportive comments to each other in front of the children. Communication between you and your ex should be cordial and should be informative about activities, medical issues, and schedules. All communication should be audio recorded or put in writing. Alternatively, both parties should use a family court–approved system for communication, such as Our Family Wizard (http://www.ourfamilywizard.com). As much as possible, the children should be protected from any ongoing animosity that reinforces the conflict and the pressure to choose. Moreover, each parent should actively promote the other parent with the message that he or she is a normative, loving parent.

Element 5: Each Parent Will Contradict the Children Should They Complain About the Other Parent

If the children complain about one parent to the other, they should be reminded that the parent about whom they are complaining is a good parent. In other words, their complaints should not be validated. The idea should be reinforced that the children do not have to choose between their parents—that they can love and be loved by both parents. Neither parent should say anything negative about the other parent to the children. Instead, the children should be encouraged to work out their issues directly with the parent involved. If the children complain to your ex about you, for example, your ex should direct the children to bring their complaints directly to you so that together you can work toward a better relationship. Any validation of their complaints will be construed as an act of interference and undermining and, hence, a violation of the court order.

Element 6: Each Parent Will Ensure That the Children Refrain from Negative Behaviors and Follow the Parenting Plan

Each parent should be held accountable for ensuring that the children are loving and respectful to the other parent. The parents should use whatever incentives, guidance, and boundaries are necessary to do so. The message to the children should be that any complaints that they have about you or your ex or any disagreements they have with you or your ex should be brought to your attention in a loving and respectful manner and/or resolved in therapy as needed. The parents should ensure that the children refrain from overtly hostile, rude, or nasty behavior, even when they are upset, and that they express their concerns in an appropriate setting and in an appropriate manner so that they can resolve them productively.

The children must be instructed to not run away from your home and seek refuge with your ex, your ex's extended family, or your ex's friends. If they do, they should not be harbored; the police must be instructed to enforce the parenting plan. If your ex facilitates the children's violation of your parenting time and/or harbors the children or arranges for them to be harbored, immediate and automatic sanctions should be implemented.

Element 7: The Children's Therapists Will Actively Support the Goal of a Positive Relationship with Both Parents

Both parents should be expressly prohibited from allowing the children to talk with any therapist/counselor without the other parent's written permission. Both parents must also refrain from discussing the possibility of therapy/counseling with the children in a blatant effort to enlist them to pressure the other parent for permission. Anyone involved in the children's mental health care and treatment must be informed about the parenting plan and should be instructed to have no contact with either parent unless absolutely necessary and not without the other parent present or being copied on the communication. That is, all communication should be shared so that there is no opportunity for either parent to undermine the therapy via private communications with the therapist. The therapist should be asked to tell the children that everything that is said during sessions is strictly confidential (with obvious limits in place for safety concerns), unless the therapy is conducted with the goal of reunification to repair a breach in the relationship. If reunification therapy is court ordered, then only a specialist in that field should be hired for that purpose.

Therapists should be asked to obtain the *I Don't Want to Choose* book and workbook (Andre and Baker 2009, available at http://www.amyjlbaker.com) and the *Welcome Back, Pluto* DVD (Warshak and Otis 2010, available at http://www.warshak.com) to use with the children as needed and appropriate. The book teaches children critical-thinking skills to allow them to resist the pressure to choose one parent over the other so that the children may love and be loved by both parents.

Therapists should avail themselves of consultations with experts on loyalty conflicts in order to ensure that they are moving toward the goal of positive and loving relationships with both parents. They should be asked to review the twelve clinical principles discussed in *Working with Alienated Children and Families: A Clinical*

Guidebook (Miller 2012) in order to ensure that they are not making fundamental clinical errors in their treatment of the children, especially the four treatment axioms: determine treatment priorities, conduct a risk/benefit analysis, provide timely and appropriate treatment, and treat the underlying condition.

Any therapists for the children or family should reinforce the concept that all parents are imperfect and should highlight the normativeness of your parenting style. Your children's distorted beliefs about you should be challenged rather than reinforced.

Element 8: Compliance with the Parenting Plan Will Be Enforced

Your proposed parenting plan should have a built-in mechanism for addressing lack of compliance. Ideally, a lack of compliance by your ex will not require a motion that your ex be held in contempt, as the process usually takes several months, and your ex would likely continue to violate the terms of the parenting plan in the meantime. Instead, the court will appoint a neutral third party, such as a parenting coordinator, who is empowered to impose sanctions (e.g., loss of time with the children) if either parent contravenes the plan. Obviously, whoever is appointed to such a position should be very familiar with the dynamics present in your case (e.g., parental alienation, false allegations of abuse, undermining and interfering behaviors) as well as fully up to speed on the history of your case. Thus, there would be no leniency. Rather than replicate the "wait and see" approach or the "it is probably a case of he said/she said" attitude that most likely contributed to the current state of affairs, the person appointed to oversee the plan would deal with any episode of noncompliance quickly and decisively. The most appropriate sanction would be loss of time with the children, not jail time or fines that would allow a wealthy parent to "buy" his way out of the plan (although a financial penalty, such as $500 per missed visit in addition to loss of time, would send a strong message).

In jurisdictions that do not allow third parties to be empowered to make modifications to the parenting plan, your attorney should have some concrete ideas for ensuring that the plan will be followed. Enforcement of the plan is just as important as the plan itself. If your ex has a history of violations of court orders, remind the court of the maxim "The best predictor of how people will behave in the future is their past behavior." Present the court with a detailed timeline of violations of prior court orders, to emphasize that unless the court does something different, your ex will disregard the new plan as well.

Exercise 9.1: Applying These Elements of a Solution to Your Situation

On a piece of paper (e.g., in a journal or notebook), copy the list of elements previously discussed:

1. Authority figures provide a clear and unambiguous expectation that the children will repair their relationship with you.

2. Each parent will refrain from interfering and undermining behaviors.

3. The favored parent will admit his role in the problem.

4. Each parent will refrain from negative communication with the other parent and actively promote the children's relationship with the other parent.

5. Each parent will contradict the children should they complain about the other parent.

6. Each parent will ensure that the children refrain from negative behaviors and follow the parenting plan.

7. The children's therapists will actively support the goal of a positive relationship with both parents.

8. Compliance with the parenting plan will be enforced.

Consider whether each one is necessary and applicable to your situation. Do you think it makes sense to include it in your proposed request? What, if anything, would you need to modify to make this work for your situation? Do you have any concerns about incorporating this element into your request? Write down your notes.

When to Seek Full Custody

As you and your attorney consider various options to put before the court (and to discuss with the custody evaluator), it is imperative that you have a clear vision of what you want to achieve. It is likely that, at some point, you will consider asking for full and complete legal and residential custody of your children, especially if the elements described above have been tried and didn't work or, for reasons outlined below, are not deemed strong enough. The court is likely to find this proposal appealing if all the following circumstances apply:

- Your ex has been found to be currently neglectful or physically or sexually abusive of the children.

- You can show a clear absence of abuse or neglect on your part.

- You had a positive relationship with your children until at least relatively recently, rather than only in the distant past.

- You have developed a reasonable plan of care for when you have full custody that takes into account your children's specific needs and demonstrates a willingness and ability to meet those needs.

- Your ex has a pattern of willful disobedience of court orders and prior efforts on your part to resolve the issues. For example, a solution has been tried and was not successful at remedying the situation.

- You show willingness to support the children's having a relationship with your ex once they have acclimated to you and under conditions in which the interference by your ex cannot begin again—for example, your ex has supervised visitation only, there is a parenting coordinator on board who has the ability to sanction your ex, or the children are clearly beyond being alienated. It is important that your proposal not appear to be an effort to take the children away from your ex forever. Otherwise, the judge will have no reason to support it. You must focus on protecting the children from abuse by your ex, coupled with protecting them from the negative long-term outcomes of the conflict. You must present your proposal as the only hope for the children to avoid those negative outcomes because it allows the children to—eventually—have a good relationship with both parents, whereas the current situation does not. You need to convey your earnest desire for the children to love and be loved by both parents.

When to Seek Full Custody Plus Intensive Reunification

When seeking full custody, it may make sense to plan to provide your children with an intensive experience that is designed to help them reunify with you in a safe and protected environment. In fact, this may be the only way to convince the judge that the transfer of custody will work. You can explain to the judge that although the children may adamantly proclaim their lack of interest in spending any time with you, the first thing you will do upon obtaining custody is enroll them in an intensive program that has a high degree of success in cases like yours. Currently there are several such programs in operation (and probably more in development) in the United States and Canada. They involve three to seven days of residence on the part of the alienated children and the targeted parent in which the children are exposed to information about undue influence (how people can be convinced of things that are not true) and trained in critical-thinking skills and ways to avoid emotional manipulation. These programs report to have a good record of repairing the relationship between alienated children and families.

There are disadvantages to this strategy, in that the program may have some bad press or could be made to appear that way by opposing counsel, or it could be an untested program that the other side can portray as extreme, radical, or dangerous. You can work with your attorney to determine how to position the program in as rational and reasoned a way as you can. Of course, it could help to remind the court that the alternative (to take a "wait and see" approach in your case) is also untested, unproven, and unvalidated. In that light, the program you propose may not seem so scary or risky. If you can get testimonials from former clients who can attest to the program's appropriateness, to the feeling of security the program engenders, and—most importantly—that the children responded to the program in a positive way, that could help the judge get past her reservations. Most courts will also want an affidavit or live testimony from the program director or at least from a recognized expert in the field to explain the therapeutic remedies in question. When researching programs, here are some questions to consider. You can enlarge the following worksheet (or download it from http://www.newharbinger.com/30734). It is important that you discuss with your attorney how and when to collect this information, because if you are not careful in your approach, your ex's attorney may complain that you "poisoned the well" by developing a one-sided relationship with the program administrators, creating a bias in the treatment. It probably makes sense for your attorney or your mental health consultant rather than you to make the inquiries with the program administrators.

Worksheet 9.1: Reunification Program Information

Basic Information

Name of program: _____

Creator/developer: _____

Year launched: _____

Location (city/state/site): _____

Is more than one family involved at a time? _____

Length of program: _____

Staffing

Will the creator/developer be running the program? _____

If not, was the person who will be running the program trained by the creator/developer?

_____

If not, by whom was the person who will be running the program trained?

_____

Names and credentials of all the people who would be working with you:

_____

In-Depth Information

Philosophy and orientation of the program:

_____

Components of the program:

_____

Is there any involvement of the favored parent? If so, what?

_____

What kind of contact can the children have with the favored parent during the program?

_____

How are the children transported to the program (if they are not cooperative)?

_____

What kind of aftercare is involved?

_____

What are the program admission criteria, and what is needed from the court (such as reversal of custody as a precondition for admission)?

_____

Admission

What is the admission process?

_____

What factors would rule a family out?

_____

Would program staff members write a letter to the court (describing their program and how you and your child represent a likely success case) if necessary?

_____

How soon after the interview/admission process is a decision made?

_____

Is there a wait list?

_____

When is the next available slot?

_____

Fees

Overall fee: _____
Does that include airfare? _____ Hotel? _____ Food? _____

What is not covered in that fee? _____

Do they take insurance? _____
Do they take installment plans? _____
Do they offer any financial aid or subsidies? _____

Effectiveness

What research has been conducted on the program?

_____

What research has been published on the program?

_____

What is the overall effectiveness rate?

_____

What factors are associated with failure of the program (are those factors present in your case)?

_____

How is success and failure defined in the research?

_____

What is the program's long-term success?

_____

Can you speak to someone who has gone through the program?

_____

Gather as much information as you can about each program you find, and propose more than one to the court so that the judge will have some options.

For some, if not all, of these programs, a requirement for admission is that the favored parent have had no contact with the children for at least ninety days. This is obviously something that the favored parent will strongly object to and claim is overly harsh and punitive. An affidavit from the program director explaining the necessity of this restriction may be very helpful, if not essential, to keep it from stalling the process.

An example of a court order transferring custody to the targeted parent appears in appendix B and is available at http://www .newharbinger.com/30734.

When to Seek Enforcement of Parenting Time and Sanctions

If your attorney strongly suspects that the judge would frown on a transfer of custody, perhaps because you have not been able to make the case that your ex is abusing your children, or if logistically a transfer of custody just does not make sense, you may choose to focus your request on *enforcement* of your parenting time, with sanctions imposed for violations. The most important aspect of this issue is *how* sanctions will be imposed. As noted above, the more immediate the sanctions are, the more likely they are to be effective. If you are required to wait six months before moving that your ex be held in contempt, your ex may not feel sufficiently incentivized to improve her behavior. Ideally, then, the sanctions will be immediate and automatic—your ex will not be provided an opportunity to make excuses or explain her behavior.

Why Not to Seek Routine Outpatient Reunification Therapy for Unjustified Rejection

It is possible that your attorney is pressuring you to seek outpatient "reunification therapy," telling you that this is the only remedy that the court is likely to support (especially if that is what the custody evaluator is strongly recommending). It is typical for the judge to order weekly parent-child therapy in cases in which children unjustifiably reject one parent and strongly align with the other, but there are several reasons routine outpatient reunification therapy is likely to be ineffective in these cases. (The word "routine" is used here to differentiate this kind of outpatient therapy from specialized outpatient reunification therapy, which we describe later in this chapter. (The word "reunification" is used to differentiate it from individual therapy.) You should present the following concerns about routine outpatient therapy to the court if necessary.

The Therapist Is Likely to "Join" with Your Children Against You

Therapists working with children who strongly (albeit unreasonably) reject a parent are prone to psychologically bonding with the children (i.e., they form a therapeutic alliance) against that parent, even if they follow element 7, to actively support the goal of a positive relationship with both parents. This is because children can be very convincing in explaining why the rejected parent is so reprehensible. People tend to assume that beliefs that are held very strongly, in this case your children's false beliefs about you, must somehow be justified. Unless the therapist is thoroughly familiar with cases like yours, she can become convinced that there is some rational and reality-based explanation for your children's rejection of you. Through the alliance with the children, the therapist can come to believe that you are to blame for the problems in the relationship. In addition, whatever contact the therapist has with your ex will probably support the children's attitude toward you. Thus, it will be natural for the therapist to join that side and assume that you are worthy of rejection.

It is also quite likely that the pressure-cooker atmosphere of the therapy, in which you would be keenly aware that the therapist is judging you, would make it even more difficult for you to be empathically attuned to your children and respond with the best possible parenting techniques. Thus, the therapist and your children would be seeing you at your worst. Rejected parents experience chronic frustration, anger, despair, and helplessness due to the ongoing interference in their relationship with their children (Baker 2006; Baker and Fine 2014b; Vassilou and Cartwright 2001). As a result, in the context of the therapy session you are likely to appear less competent than you really are, increasing the likelihood that the therapist will conclude that the rejection is deserved.

Also working against you is the fact that most therapists are trained to accept, support, and advocate for their clients' needs. Most therapists work with their clients' perceptions, rather than attempting to determine the factual accuracy of those perceptions by speaking with "collateral contacts" and using other information-gathering methods. This promotes a supportive atmosphere, but may also lead therapists to be reluctant to actively challenge a client's assumptions and interpretations. This may be why rejected parents often report that parent-child therapy was harmful, not helpful, and that the therapist "made things worse." Although courts often view this as evidence that the rejected parent lacks understanding or does not "get it," it is quite possible—perhaps even more likely—that it is the therapist who lacks understanding and does not "get it," and that the rejected parent was in a no-win double bind.

Some therapists are trained to assume that children would never lie about something as serious as abuse. Although many children tell the truth about their abuse experiences, some do not. To the extent that the therapist does join with your children against you, the children will become further entrenched in and committed to their position, which could be harmful for your relationship with them.

The Children Would Still Be Exposed to Negative Messages About You

While seeing you in routine outpatient therapy, your children would still be spending most of their time with their other parent and would still be exposed to that parent's messages that support their rejection of you (unless the court has implemented the elements previously described). They would be interacting with people who support their position (i.e., your ex's family members and friends) and presented with a version of reality in which you are the villain and your ex is the hero. A part of their ongoing life experience would still be consistent with the belief that you are unworthy and should be avoided or discarded. If you imagine your children as belonging to a cult that worships your ex, routine outpatient therapy is like offering them a weekly deprogramming session and then returning them to the cult for the remainder of the week. Typically, for deprogramming to be effective, a cult member needs to be removed from the cult altogether. The cult's message is so powerful that even the smallest exposure to the ideology of the cult can eradicate the individual's ability to think critically and be true to herself. Likewise, it is unlikely that the effect of your ex's negative messages can be undone in hour-long weekly sessions while the children are still immersed in an environment that supports their rejection of you. Your children's relationship with your ex may be so powerful and all-encompassing for them that it would be virtually impossible for them to experience you independent of your ex's perceptions of you. They would be unable to form independent thoughts, feelings, and needs outside of their enmeshed relationship with your ex.

The Process of Therapy May Encourage or Force Your Children to "Make Their Case"

Weekly therapy may also devolve into a hate session in which your children are encouraged and/or allowed to enumerate the many reasons you deserve their contempt and rejection. This exercise alone could deepen their disaffection for you, as they become increasingly convinced of the righteousness of their position. Knowing that the therapist is an authority on the case might lead your ex to coach the children to present their best case against you. If the therapist allows this "free-for-all" to continue, it may further damage your relationship with your children.

The Treatment Implies You Are the Problem

The court's determination that *you and your children* (as opposed to your ex and the children, or you, your ex, and the children) need therapy together sends the message that the problem is the relationship between you and your children. In essence, the court is endorsing the view that *you* are the cause of the breach in the relationship. The judge (the ultimate authority in these proceedings) has deemed you to be "the problem" and your ex innocent of any wrongdoing. Your ex is completely "off the hook" for any of the difficulties your children and you are experiencing.

Your children will hear this message loud and clear. Even before the first session is held, this message reinforces beliefs they hold that will undermine improvements or progress that could be made in therapy with you. Even if your children had been inclined to question your ex's perspective on you, they are now less likely to, as the judge has implied that such questioning is not warranted.

But, it is not just the children who receive this message. Your ex, you, and the therapist are receiving it as well. To the extent that favored parents are arrogant and perceive themselves to be above reproach, this legal intervention will bolster your ex's arrogance and unwillingness to cooperate with you. To the extent that you feel blamed and ashamed, being mandated into treatment that implies you are the problem may increase your sense of demoralization and hopelessness. A therapist is even more likely to join with a child client (see element 7) when only one parent is mandated for treatment.

It Is Unlikely That Your Ex Will Comply

The final reason routine outpatient therapy between your children and you would be insufficient is that it places all the scheduling and attendance power in the hands of the parent least likely to support the therapy. It is unlikely that your ex will actually deliver the children to the therapy sessions, especially if the therapist appears to be in support of their reconciliation with you and/or focuses on your ex's behavior. If your case is severe enough that your children have no contact with you outside of therapy, the full responsibility of delivering your children to the therapy sessions falls on your ex, a person who is not likely to be supportive of improving the children's relationship with you. More likely, unless the elements above are included in the court order and enforced, your ex will stall, delay, and avoid therapy by citing conflicting schedules, prior commitments, illnesses, and the children's own lack of interest in the therapy.

No matter what they may say, most favored parents do not really want the children to have a healthy and active relationship with the other parent, nor do they want their behaviors to be scrutinized in therapy. Reunification therapy represents a challenge to their control and to their place as the primary, if not only, authority in the children's lives. Therefore, your ex has every reason to undermine and sabotage the therapy. Putting your ex in charge of delivering the children to the sessions is asking her to go against her own self-interest, something she is unlikely to do.

Specialized Outpatient Reunification Therapy

The primary reason routine outpatient therapy is likely to be insufficient, and perhaps even detrimental, is that anyone can claim to be a reunification therapist. Too often, people with no real experience or understanding of the dynamics involved take these cases and mismanage them because they endorse a model in which the rejected parent is viewed as the cause of the children's disaffection.

Fortunately, there are some true outpatient reunification specialists who have written about their programs, and if one of them (or someone who has trained with them or follows their protocol) is available to you, then outpatient reunification therapy could be an acceptable resolution for your case (Baker and Sauber 2012). Essential elements of these programs include the following:

- First and foremost, an experienced mental health professional who truly understands the difference between justified and unjustified rejection and is not distracted by your normative flaws, your children's false claims, or your ex's obfuscation and lack of compliance

- A tried and true structured therapeutic protocol (not simply weekly sessions in which the children air their grievances)

    What is called for is a psychoeducational intervention, rather than insight-oriented talk therapy. Within the protocol should be milestones and objective markers of success and a very clear expectation that within a relatively short period of time the children and the rejected parent will be reunified.

○ A willingness and ability to work closely with the courts, to invoke the law to enforce compliance among recalcitrant favored parents who have no obvious reason to comply with the therapeutic schedule and will most likely work diligently to undermine it

Another element in at least some of the better known programs is the use of a one-way mirror (so that the children can observe the parent without being seen) to allow the children to acclimate to the rejected parent in a safe and incremental fashion. See *Working with Alienated Children and Families: A Clinical Guidebook* (Baker and Sauber 2012) for a description of three such programs.

Additional Considerations

There are three additional issues to consider when putting together your list of requests of the court. The first pertains to children's lawyers/advocates. In some jurisdictions, the court can appoint a lawyer or advocate for the children, if a parent requests it. In order to know whether you may want to ask for a lawyer/advocate for your children or, alternatively, oppose a motion by your ex asking for one, it is essential that you understand that jurisdictions vary as to the role of these professionals. In some jurisdictions, this person is merely a mouthpiece for the children, stating their position for the court. Such children's advocates tend to work hand in hand with the favored parent's attorney, as their interests coincide. In other jurisdictions, the professional representing a child is allowed to override the child's stated wishes if those wishes are deemed to be not in the child's best interest.

It will also be helpful to know that in some jurisdictions, once children are of a certain age, they are allowed to have a say in their custody and parenting plan. This information can be found in the best interest of the child (BIC) statutes, listed by jurisdiction in the appendix. If your children are too young to have a say, your attorney should incorporate that fact into your proposed remedy.

Finally, many judges prefer to maintain the status quo rather than impose a plan that would go against the children's stated desires. Again, there is a built-in bias toward keeping things the way they are. Whatever remedy you are asking for will likely fall outside the judge's comfort zone. Therefore, your attorney (and any experts you hire) should be well prepared to present a rational and compelling case for why the court must do something. For the judge to entertain any remedy that you propose, you must argue and show that choosing to do nothing (i.e., letting nature take its course) has the potential to contribute to long-term negative consequences for the children.

Summary

At some point in your custody case, you will need to put forth a plan for how to proceed. A bulletproof plan will be well thought out and made with your children's best interest foremost in your mind. Most likely, you will need to involve the services of mental health professionals. When doing so, make sure that they are seasoned professionals with extensive experience with cases like yours and that there is a mechanism for the court to enforce the parenting plan you propose, should that be required.

APPENDIX A

List of Statutes Pertaining to the Best Interest of the Child

IN THE UNITED STATES:

Alabama: Title 30, chapter 3, article 1

Alaska: Title 25, chapter 24, section 150

Arizona: Title 25, chapter 4, article 1, section 403

Arkansas: Title 9, subtitle 2, chapter 13, subchapter 1, section 101

California: Division 8, part 2, chapter 2, sections 3040–49

Colorado: Chapter 87, section 1, subsection 14-10-124

Connecticut: Chapter 815j, section 46b-56

Delaware: Title 13, chapter 7, subchapter 2, section 722

Florida: Title VI, chapter 61, section 61.13

Georgia: Title 19, chapter 9, article 1

Hawaii: Division 3, title 31, chapter 571, part 5, section 46

Idaho: Title 32, chapter 7, section 717

Illinois: Chapter 40, part 6, section 601

Indiana: Title 31, article 17, chapter 2, section 31-17-2-8

Iowa: Title XV, subtitle 1, chapter 598, section 41

Kansas: Chapter 23, article 32, section 3

Kentucky: Title XXXV, chapter 403, section 270

Louisiana: Book 1, title V, chapter 2, section 3, article 134

Maine: Title 9-A, chapter 694, part B, section 2, part E, section 2, part 3, chapter 55, section 1653

Maryland: Family Law Title 5 and Title 9

Massachusetts: Title 3, chapter 208, section 31

Michigan: Chapter 722, Act 91 of 1970, section 722.23

Minnesota: Chapter 518, section 155

Mississippi: Title 93, chapter 5, section 24

Missouri: Chapter 452, section 375

Montana: Title 40, chapter 4, section 212

Nebraska: Chapter 43, section 2923

Nevada: Chapter 125, section 480

New Hampshire: Chapter 461-A, section 461-A:6

New Jersey: Title 9, chapter 2, section 4

New Mexico: Chapter 40, article 4, section 40-4-9

New York: Domestic relations law 70

North Carolina: Chapter 50, article 1, section 50-13.2

North Dakota: Chapter 14-09, section 5, 14-09-06.2

Ohio: Title 31, chapter 31-09.04

Oklahoma: Title 43, section 109.3

Oregon: Volume 3, chapter 107, section 107.137

Pennsylvania: Chapter 53, subchapter A, section 5328

Rhode Island: Title 15, chapter 15-5, section 15-5-16

South Carolina: Title 63, chapter 15, article 1, section 16-15-240

South Dakota: Chapter 25-4, section 45

Tennessee: Title 36, chapter 6, part 1, section 36-6-106

Texas: Title 5, subtitle B, chapter 153, section 153.001, chapters A–E

Utah: Title 30, chapter 3, section 10

Vermont: Title 15, chapter 11, section 665

Virginia: Title 20, chapter 6.1, section 20-124.3

Washington: Title 26, chapter 26.09, section 26. 09.187

Washington, DC: Section 16-2353

West Virginia: Chapter 48, article 9, section 102

Wisconsin: Act 9, section 767.41

Wyoming: Title 20, chapter 2, article 2, section 201

IN CANADA:

Federal: Federal Divorce Act RSC 1985, c3

Alberta: Family Law Act, SA 2003, c F-4.5

British Columbia: Family Law Act SBC 2011

Manitoba: Family Maintenance Act, CCSM c F20

New Brunswick: Family Services Act, SNB 1980, c F-2.2

Newfoundland and Labrador: RSNL 1990, c C-13

Northwest Territories: Children's Law Act SNWT 1997

Nova Scotia: Maintenance and Custody Act, RSNS 1989, c 160

Nunavut: Children's Law Act SNWT (Nu) 1997

Ontario: Children's Law Reform Act RSO 1990, c C.12

Prince Edward Island: Custody Jurisdiction and Enforcement Act, RSPEI 1988, c C-33

Quebec: Civil Code of Quebec, LRQ, c C-1991

Saskatchewan: The Children's Law Act, 1997, SS 1997, c C-8.2

Yukon: Child and Family Services Act, RSY 2002, c 31

APPENDIX B

Example of a Court Order Transferring Custody to the Targeted Parent

1. Case Management

The parties shall request an Order of the Local Administrative Judge that a justice be appointed to Case Manage this case for one year after the date of these minutes of settlement unless further extended by Order of the Court.

2. Parental Coordinator

2.1. The parties' co-parenting will be assisted by the services of a parental coordinator (the "PC"), who will have a mediation and parental advice mandate. The parental coordinator shall be selected by the reconciliation therapist if the parties cannot agree.

2.2. The PC shall be appointed by the parties for the purpose of assisting the parties' co-parenting of their children in accordance with the prevailing custody/access Orders and fostering compliance with such Orders. The Parental Coordinator shall be compellable as a witness in the event of any litigated dispute regarding custody/access.

3. Parenting—Ancillary Matters

3.1. The parties shall ensure that when the other parent calls, the children will return messages within a 24-hour period. All phone calls between the children and the other parent shall be private and not on speaker phone, and neither parent shall permit anyone else, including their extended family, to listen in on such calls.

3.2. The parents shall each maintain a working telephone with an answering machine/service and email. The parents agree to keep each other informed of all current phone numbers and email addresses (and the cell phone and email and social networking addresses of the children, as applicable) and shall notify each other in writing of any changes. Communications between each parent and the children shall not be intercepted or read by, or on behalf of, the other parent. The Parental Coordinator shall be entitled, should he consider it advisable, to review parent-child electronic communications.

3.3. The parents shall be provided with copies of school pictures for the children that they have not previously been provided with and copies of such family mementoes, school reports, extra-curricular activities' pictures and awards and similar child-focused items as they may reasonably request, at the requesting parent's cost.

3.4. Each parent will be given access to all schedules for the children's extra-curricular activities, including but not limited to soccer, music, dance, gymnastics and acting lessons. The parents' contact information will be given to all activity coordinators so that they can be sent all information pertaining to such activities.

3.5. Each parent shall provide the other with the names, addresses and phone numbers of all health care professionals (physicians, dentists, orthodontists, etc.) providing care, or who might be used to provide care, to the children (such as a walk-in-clinic in each parent's neighborhood).

3.6. Each parent shall provide the other with copies of any medical and/or professional reports, etc. she or he may have pertaining to the children. The parents may also request any relevant records/information from the children's professionals directly. If required by the physician, the parents shall provide written permission to the child's physician to release information to the other parent.

3.7. The parents shall promptly notify each other of any potential non-routine or major medical decisions. The parents shall provide each other with the name and telephone number of the attending practitioners. The parents shall both consult with the relevant physicians and attempt to come to a mutual decision about major medical issues in accordance with consensus professional opinion. The parents shall rely on the children's pediatrician/physician for assistance in organizing the various referrals, assimilating the information and opinions and in coming to the final decision. In the unlikely event there is no consensus professional opinion after following the above procedures, the Applicant's decision will prevail.

3.8. The parents shall notify each other as soon as feasible, immediately if possible, of an emergency visit to a physician, specialist, and/or hospital. Both parents may attend.

3.9. A school calendar is available from each school. It is each parent's responsibility to stay up to date on any relevant educational matters (professional activity days, special events, field trips, concerts, parent-teacher meetings, etc.).

3.10. Each parent shall request from the schools that he/she be provided with all the notices, communications, flyers, report cards, etc. In the event that only one parent is in receipt of same, including report cards (and typically including notice and forms brought home from school), such parent shall immediately upon receipt forward a copy of same, or full details of same, to the other parent by fax or email. Each parent shall provide the other with whatever consents are required for full, timely and equal access to information regarding the children.

3.11. Each parent will be permitted to meet with the children's teachers and other instructors to discuss educational and developmental progress.

3.12. The parents shall discuss, in a timely way, forthcoming major issues regarding changes at school and at school programs. Each shall advise the other if the school calls regarding a significant child-related matter. There is no change of school, other than through graduation, anticipated or expected.

3.13. Mutual consent of both parents is required if the activity overlaps into both parents' time and/or if the involvement of both parents is required. One parent, with the other parent's permission, can be responsible for an activity that overlaps the other parent's time. If these matters cannot be settled, the parties shall refer the matter to the Parental Coordinator.

3.14. The parents shall provide each other with all necessary information regarding the children's activities and lessons regardless of whose time the activity falls on.

3.15. If the resident parent cannot take the child to a scheduled activity/lesson, the non-resident parent may be given the option to do so if this works out best for all concerned. This is a choice and not a first right of refusal; the resident parent may make other arrangements for the children to attend.

3.16. Both parents and their families may attend the special events associated with lessons and activities. Both parents and their families may also attend the children's sports practices, recitals, performances, games, and other activities or lessons.

3.17. The Applicant shall hold the children's vaccination records, birth certificates, and passports and provide photocopies (notarized if necessary) regularly to the Respondent upon request. Each parent shall ensure that the required or necessary documentation shall accompany the children when they travel out of town overnight, as when requested by the parent traveling with the children.

3.18. If a parent travels (without the child), he/she shall provide in writing, a phone number to the resident parent in case of a child-related emergency and/or if the child wants to contact the traveling parent.

3.19. The location(s) and phone number(s) of the children's whereabouts when traveling away from either parent's residence overnight shall be provided to the other parent in writing, prior to departure, in case of an emergency.

3.20. Where either parent intends to travel outside the jurisdiction with the children, he/she will give at least two weeks' written notice to the other parent. Provided, however, that day-trips shall require only 24 hours' notice to the other parent.

3.21. The written consent required by law, the written authorizations, documents and approvals required by passport, border, immigration, travel and other authorities to effect such approved travels, and the necessary papers such as the traveling child's passport, health certificates, vaccination papers, and birth certificate shall be provided forthwith by the non-traveling parent, when requested. The non-traveling parent shall receive a full itinerary of the trip.

3.22. The parents shall not record, by audio, video or other means inter-parent or parent-child conversations. The parents shall not permit or acquiesce in the children making any such recordings either.

4. Special Days and Holidays

4.1. If a parent is the non-residential parent, such parent shall be entitled to visit with the children on the parent's birthday and Fathers' Day or Mothers' Day as the case may be, from 9:00 a.m. until 7:30 p.m.

4.2. The non-residential parent shall celebrate the children's birthdays with them on the immediately preceding or the immediately following day (or such other day as the parent may select) that they are the residential parent.

4.3. All school holidays shall be shared equally by the parents, including the Christmas, March and summer breaks. The PC shall work with the parents on allocating such school-break time equitably.

5. Miscellaneous Provisions—Custody and Access

5.1. Both parents and their families may attend open houses, school council meetings, curriculum night, plays, concerts, and assemblies, fundraisers, camp visitors' days, organized sports games and practices, and other functions, regardless of the residential schedule.

5.2. If either parent dies, it is the intention that the other parent shall become the sole custodial parent of the children and if either parent makes a will or other testamentary document, the guardianship provisions shall provide that the other parent shall be the guardian of the children and entitled to sole decision-making authority.

5.3. Each parent shall be entitled to have a full and active role in providing a sound moral, social, economic and educational environment for the children. The custodial or decision-making or access powers shall only be exercised in a way that is in the best interests of the children. Neither parent shall make any statement nor take any action with the intent or effect of portraying the other parent as marginalized in the life of the children because they are not the "custodial" parent. Rather, each parent shall in all communications to or relating to the children message that both parents are to be considered full and involved parents in the children's lives.

5.4. Each of the parents shall exert every effort to maintain free access to an unhampered contact between the children and the other parent and to foster a feeling of affection between the children and the other parent. Neither parent shall speak to, or in the presence of, the children in a derogatory manner concerning the other parent, or permit anyone else to do so. Neither parent shall do anything which would estrange the children from the other; which would injure the opinion of the children as to their mother or father; or which would impair the natural development of the children's love and response for each of the parents. Specifically, each parent shall continue to communicate to, and foster in, the children a concept of the other parent as safe, loving, and available and a belief that each parent (i) can make a substantial contribution to the upbringing of each of the children, (ii) is supportive of the children's relationship with both parents and (iii) is fully supportive of the terms of this settlement as being in the best interests of the children.

5.5. The parents shall not share or discuss with the children inter-parental communications or disputes, nor shall they permit anyone else to do so.

5.6. If either parent has any concerns regarding the care of the children while they are in the care of the other parent, they shall first raise them with the Parental Coordinator and seek his advice prior to raising them with the Police, child protection authorities or others.

6. Non-Compliance with Access and Other Parental and Child Behavior Issues

6.1. The parents shall be required to utilize all appropriate incentives and consequences, guidance and boundaries, on an urgent and escalating basis, so as to require the children to comply with the living arrangements and other parental contact prescribed by Court Order and as recommended by the Parental Coordinator and Therapist.

6.2. If, in the opinion of a qualified mental health professional, after consultations with the parties' Parental Coordinator, that the parenting plan contained herein is not being implemented successfully, either the Applicant or the Respondent may return this matter to Court for a review of custody and access and further relief to protect the children's right to a relationship with both parents. There shall not be a need to demonstrate a further material change of circumstances prior to returning this matter to Court.

6.3. If this matter is returned to Court for a review by either party, the trial Judge shall have discretion to deal with all the costs incurred throughout this case.

6.4. Parental and child behaviors to be expected and enforced include the following:

a. Civility, mutual respect and courtesy

b. Respect for appropriate generational boundaries

c. School homework and attendance and related responsibilities of the children to their school is a priority and each parent shall appropriately supervise and monitor the children's performance and work habits and related bedtimes and activities.

d. The children shall treat each other with respect and courtesy. Bullying and other emotionally abusive behavior shall not be tolerated.

e. Travel consent letters shall be provided on a timely basis.

f. Self-help remedies contrary to the terms of the settlement and parenting plan shall not be tolerated.

g. Neither parent should accept any assertion from the children that an activity will not be attended should the other parent attend.

h. Neither parent shall demand that the other not show up to the children's activities.

i. Each parent shall be informed on a timely manner of all the children's activities.

j. Both parents will be listed directly with all the children's third party activities such as sports teams, dance and other extra-curricular activities. Both parents will be promptly notified of games, practices and activities.

k. Neither parent shall permit or tolerate the children while in his/her presence not greeting the other parent, and neither parent is to cross the street with the children in order to avoid the other parent.

l. When the parties come into contact with each other, they are not to shield the children from the view of either parent with the intent or the effect of avoiding interaction with the child or the other parent.

m. When either parent is exercising telephone access, the following applies:

n.   Neither parent is to record telephone calls between the other parent and the children.

1.   Both parents must ensure that the other parent's telephone calls are being answered and not screening the calls to the answering machine.

2.   Neither parent is to ignore and withhold the other parent's messages for the children.

3.   The children must be given privacy when speaking to either parent.

4.   Both parents must provide parental expectation on the children when they are to engage in telephone calls with the other parent.

o.   The residential parent must ensure that the children are in receipt of and acknowledge greeting cards and gifts being sent by the other parent.

p.   The parties are not to discuss financial issues with the children.

q.   The parties are to inform each other of the children's medical appointments and health care providers.

r.   The parties are to inform each other of when the children are ill and missing school.

s.   The parties are responsible for bringing the children to the reunification therapist appointments. The parties' schedules are not to be used as an excuse for non-attendance.

t.   The parties are to inform each other of all the prescription medication being taken by the children.

u.   Both parties will demonstrate equal love and affection to all the children and promote in the children a view that they are all equally loved.

v. The parties are to provide travel consent letters and mandatory guidance and boundaries that children will vacation with the other parent.

w. If a child attends at the residence of the non-residential parent instead of the residential parent, the non-residential parent shall forthwith deliver and/or arrange for the child to be delivered to the residential parent.

x. Neither party will authorize, permit or acquiesce in the children being disrespectful to the other parent, and each parent will take the appropriate action at their own home to support the parent who is being treated disrespectfully by the children.

y. The parties shall ensure that the children's homework is completed before they are allowed to commence other activities, such as going on the computer or playing games.

z. The parties are to make sure that items from the other parent's home will not be taken by the children.

References

American Psychological Association. 2012. *Guidelines for Child Custody Evaluations in Family Law Proceedings.* Washington, DC: Author. https://www.apa.org/practice/guidelines/child-custody.pdf.

Andre, K., and A.J.L. Baker. 2009. *I Don't Want to Choose: How Middle School Kids Can Avoid Choosing One Parent over the Other.* New York: Kindred Spirits.

Association of Family and Conciliation Courts. 2006. *Model Standards of Practice for Child Custody Evaluations.* Madison, WI: Author. http://www.afccnet.org/Portals/0/ModelStdsChildCustodyEvalSept2006.pdf.

Baker, A.J.L. 2006. "The Power of Stories: Stories About Power: Why Therapists and Clients Should Read Stories About the Parental Alienation Syndrome." *American Journal of Family Therapy* 34: 191–203.

———. 2007. *Adult Children of Parental Alienation Syndrome: Breaking the Ties That Bind.* New York: W.W. Norton.

———. 2010. "Even When You Win You Lose: Disfavored Parents' Perceptions of Their Attorneys." *American Journal of Family Therapy* 38: 1–18.

Baker, A.J.L., and D. Darnall. 2006. "Behaviors and Strategies of Parental Alienation: A Survey of Parental Experiences." *Journal of Divorce and Remarriage* 45: 97–124.

Baker, A.J.L., and P. Fine. 2014a. *Co-parenting with a Toxic Ex: Protecting Your Child from Loyalty Conflicts and Alienation.* Oakland, CA: New Harbinger Publications.

————. 2014b. *Surviving Parental Alienation: Journeys of Hope and Healing.* Lanham, MD: Rowman & Littlefield.

Baker, A.J.L., and S. R. Sauber (eds.). 2012. *Working with Alienated Children and Families: A Clinical Guidebook.* New York: Routledge.

Bathurst, K., A. W. Gottfried, and A. E. Gottfried. 1997. "Normative Data for the MMPI-2 in Child Custody Litigation." *Psychological Assessment* 9: 205–11.

Bone, J. M., and S. R. Sauber. 2012. "The Essential Role of the Mental Health Consultant in Parental Alienation Cases." In *Working with Alienated Children and Families: A Clinical Guidebook,* edited by A.J.L. Baker and S. R. Sauber. New York: Routledge.

Federal Rules of Evidence. 2010. Washington, DC: US Government Printing Office. http://www.uscourts.gov/uscourts/rulesandpolicies/rules/2010%20rules/evidence.pdf

————. 1998. *Parental Alienation Syndrome: A Guide for Legal and Mental Health Professionals.* Cresskill, NJ: Creative Therapeutics Inc.

Harvard Mental Health Newsletter. 2011. "In Praise of Gratitude." Cambridge, MA: Harvard Medical School. http://www.health.harvard.edu/newsletters/Harvard_Mental_Health_Letter/2011/November/in-praise-of-gratitude.

Miller, S. 2012. "Clinical Reasoning and Clinical Decision Making in Cases of Severe Child Alignment: Diagnostic and Therapeutic Issues." In *Working with Alienated Children and Families: A Clinical Guidebook,* edited by A.J.L. Baker and S. R. Sauber. New York: Routledge.

National Center for Complementary and Alternative Medicine. 2011. *Relaxation Techniques for Health: An Introduction* (fact sheet). N.p.: US Department of Human Health and Services. http://nccam.nih.gov/sites/nccam.nih.gov/files/relaxation_introduction.pdf.

Vassilou, D., and G. Cartwright. 2001. "The Lost Parents' Perspective on Parental Alienation Syndrome." *American Journal of Family Therapy* 29: 181–91.

Warshak, R. A., and M. R. Otis. 2010. *Welcome Back, Pluto: Understanding, Preventing, and Overcoming Parental Alienation.* Directed by Tracy Ready. US: Trace Productions for WBP Media. DVD, 83 mins.

Amy J. L. Baker, PhD, has a doctorate in developmental psychology from Teachers College, Columbia University, and is a professional writer and researcher. She is the author of *Adult Children of Parental Alienation Syndrome* and coauthor of *Co-parenting with a Toxic Ex*, among other books and articles on parental alienation and parent-child relationships.

J. Michael Bone, PhD, has a doctorate from the Graduate Faculty of Political and Social Science of the New School for Social Research in New York, NY. He has served as a mental health expert, consultant, and advisor to the court on parental alienation cases around the United States, and maintains a consulting practice in Florida.

Brian Ludmer, BComm, LLB, is an attorney whose practice is based in Toronto, Ontario, Canada. He has a Bachelor of Commerce (1982) and Bachelor of Law (1985) from the University of Toronto. Ludmer has practiced corporate and securities law for twenty-seven years and in parallel he conducts a family law practice focused on situations involving custody disputes, child estrangement, and parental alienation, as well as high net worth divorce litigation and business valuation.

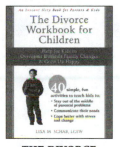
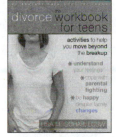